THE LAW OF STUDENT EXPULSIONS AND SUSPENSIONS

SECOND EDITION

Lawrence F. Rossow
Professor of Education
and Adjunct Professor of Law
The University of Oklahoma

and

Jerry R. Parkinson
Dean of the College of Law
The University of Wyoming

Disclaimer

The Education Law Association (ELA) is a private, nonadvocacy, and nonprofit association of educators and attorneys. The opinions expressed in this publication are those of the authors and do not represent official views of the Association.

ISBN 1-56534-071-X

Published by
Education Law Association
300 College Park, Dayton, Ohio 45469-2280
(937) 229-3589
ela@udayton.edu
www.educationlaw.org

About the Authors

Lawrence F. Rossow is a Professor of Education and Adjunct Professor of Law at the University of Oklahoma. At the University of Oklahoma, he is responsible for teaching and research in the College of Education as well as the College of Law and is former Chair of the Department of Educational Leadership and Policy Studies.

He is the author of six books and more than 50 articles concerning topics in education law. In addition to his publishing activities, he serves on the editorial board of four national journals and is a grant reviewer for the U.S. Department of Education.

He is the editor of the *School Law Reporter*, a monthly publication of the Education Law Association.

In 1995, Professor Rossow was the keynote speaker at the first international education law conference for the Republic of South Africa and in 1996 delivered the keynote address for the Australia and New Zealand Education Law Association Convention.

Professor Rossow received his doctorate in Educational Administration, specializing in education, from Loyola University of Chicago where he studied at the School of Education and School of Law. Prior to becoming a professor, he spent 13 years as a school administrator and teacher. Professor Rossow has been a principal and superintendent and has taught both at the elementary and high school levels. His experience spans inner-city, urban, suburban and rural schools.

Jerry R. Parkinson is Dean of the College of Law at the University of Wyoming in Laramie. From 1987 until 1998, he was a member of the faculty at the University of Oklahoma College of Law, where he also served as Associate Dean from 1992 until 1996. Dean Parkinson is the author of numerous articles and other publications, primarily in the area of education law. He served five years as co-editor of the *School Law Reporter*, a monthly publication of the Education Law Association. He received his J.D. Degree from the University of Iowa and is a member of the American Bar Association, the Oregon State Bar, and the Education Law Association.

Acknowledgment

The authors wish to thank Dr. Nancy D. Rossow, Marie Eileen Rossow, Deb Parkinson, and Dr. Frances Paterson for their help and support during this project.

Table of Contents

INTRODUCTION

In 1975 the U.S. Supreme Court decided *Goss v. Lopez,* which provided the foundation for the law of procedure in student suspensions.[1] Since *Goss,* hundreds of student suspension cases have been decided. Taken together, these cases shape the body of law for expulsion and suspension in American public schools. The purpose of this book is to outline, describe, and interpret the law of student expulsion and suspension as it is known today.

The primary focus will be on procedural aspects, although an overview of the issues surrounding substantive due process is included. The book will be devoted to the elementary and secondary public school settings involving regular education students. Both higher education and special education student expulsions and suspensions have become unique activities for which the reader should consult other treatises.

The Fourteenth Amendment

The constitutional basis for due process for students can be traced to the Fourteenth Amendment. It states in part that "No state ... shall deprive any person of life, liberty, or property, without due process of law...." The *Goss* decision established that a student's education is a *property interest.*[2] The *Goss* Court also held that when a student is suspended, a student's liberty interest is implicated. For legal purposes, public schools are considered "the state" and thus can't suspend a student with out first providing the student with due process.

The recording of the suspension in the student's file could have serious ramifications on the student's future education. Any activity of the state (school) that results in the possible damage to a citizen's (student's) good name, honor, or reputation implicates a liberty interest. The presence of a liberty interest requires that due process be provided.

---

[1] 419 U.S. 565 (1975).

[2] *Id.* at 574.

The Concept of Due Process

Defining due process of law can be extremely difficult. The Supreme Court commented several decades ago: "Due process is an elusive concept. Its exact boundaries are undefinable, and its content varies according to specific factual contexts...whether the Constitution requires that a particular right obtained in a specific proceeding depends upon a complexity of factors.[3]

Defining Minimum Due Process - *Goss v. Lopez*

Prior to 1975, the courts did not recognize the need to provide due process for students who were suspended for short periods of time. However, the definition of "short-term" and "long-term" was not universal. A specified number of days of suspension in one state (15 days for example) might be viewed as a short-term suspension. The same number of days in another state could be viewed as a long-term suspension.

In addition to the lack of quantitative indices for short-term/ long-term suspensions, what constituted due process for even long-term suspensions was not always clear. Perhaps it was fortunate for the Court that the *Goss* case involved the suspension of students without due process for ten days. This period of time for which the students were suspended plus the absence of any due process gave the Court the opportunity to provide quantitative guidelines to answer the questions *when* and *how much* due process was due.

For students involved in a ten-day or less suspension, the Court said, "At the very minimum...students facing suspension and the consequent interference with a protected property interest must be given some kind of notice and afforded some kind of hearing" and that "Longer suspensions or expulsions for the remainder of the school term, or permanently, may require more formal procedures."[4]

---

[3] Lawrence F. Rossow, *Administrative Discretion and Student Suspensions: A Lion In Waiting*, 13 J.L. & Educ. 418-19 (1984).
[4] 419 U.S. at 579.

The holding sent a message to all states that henceforth suspensions of ten days or less are of the short-term variety and require a minimum due process procedure of notice and informal hearing. Suspensions of more than ten days require more notice and an informal hearing. While the *Goss* decision focused on short-term suspensions, it helped shape the guidelines for all suspensions. As a result, school authorities can distinguish between short-term and long-term suspension and determine more precisely how much due process may be due a student facing sanction.

LONG-TERM SUSPENSIONS AND EXPULSIONS

The distinction between a long-term suspension and expulsion is mainly length of time. An expulsion is the term most commonly used for a permanent removal from school. A long-term suspension refers to any suspension over ten days. A number of states do not permit expulsions. For example, Oklahoma places a cap on the number of days of suspension. The statute notes that the suspension "shall not extend beyond the current semester and the succeeding semester."[5] An expulsion may take place, in effect, if another governmental agency assumes responsibility for the student, i.e. juvenile justice. It could be envisioned that if a student were to be found guilty of a capital crime, he would be schooled while incarcerated. He would of course not be in attendance at the local public school.

Alabama is one state that does permit the permanent removal of a student by the decision of the local school board. However, there appears to be some need to coordinate with juvenile court because the offense committed, while a violation of a school rule, is typically a violation of the criminal code as well.[6]

Whether long-term suspension or expulsion, the due process will be the same. Once the number of days of the punishment moves from the ten-days-or-less to the over-ten-day category, it requires formal rather than informal procedures. The case law does not support any further distinctions.

---

[5] Okla. Stat. Ann. tit. 70 sec. 24.101.3 (West Supp. 1997).

[6] Scoggins v. Henry County Board of Education, 549 So.2d 99 (Ala. Civ. App. 1989).

The requirements of *Goss v. Lopez* are constitutional minimums and apply only to short-term suspensions. States or local school boards may offer additional procedural protections for students during the suspension process be it long or short term. However, once the local board elects to provide more than the minimum due process, the courts will expect the board to observe those additional protections.

Just assuming minimum due process, the specifics of the long-term suspension or expulsion are not as clear cut as they are for the short-term suspension since there is not a U.S. Supreme Court *Goss* counterpart for the longer school separations.[7]

In this section the many issues surrounding the providing of procedural due process for students facing long-term suspension and expulsion will be examined. School authorities may agree that such protections as notice, formal hearing, and representation by counsel are necessary. However, it is the interpretation of these procedural requisites that creates problems. A synthesis of the case law since the 1970s shows where schools have made legal errors and where their suspension practices have sustained the challenges.

Notice

To exist, due process must meet the requirement of notice. First, some clearly understood school rule must forewarn the student that certain behavior might result in expulsion.[8]

However, the exact form of the rules seems flexible. In one case, a student was suspended for distributing vulgar material in school. The school claimed that statements on the cover and in the introductory section of the student handbook provided sufficient notice to the student that this type of behavior was punishable by suspension. However, these remarks did not specifically mention the student's actions. The First Circuit Court of Appeals held that the rules of the school had adequately informed the student.[9]

In addition to being informed as to which behavior will lead to suspension, the student and parents must be given a statement of specific charges and grounds that, if proven, could lead to the long-term suspension.

---

[7] Goss, 419, U.S. 565

[8] Arrington v. Eberhart, 920 F. Supp. 1208 (M.D. Ala.1996).

[9] Donovan v. Ritchie, 68 F.3d 14 (1st Cir. 1995).

Many state statutes require that parents receive written notice. In Illinois, for example, school officials must provide a written notice to parents by "registered or certified mail." An Illinois Association of School Boards' publication recommends that a copy of the intent to expel notice also be sent by regular mail as a precaution against registered or certified mail being refused. A question may arise concerning notice when parents are divorced. Which parent should be contacted? Generally the custodial parent with whom the school has established a relationship should receive the notice. In cases where both parents seem to participate in the child's education, i.e. both attend conferences, volunteer for chaperoning, etc., it might be wise for school officials to contact both parents. Certainly, the school must contact both parents when joint custody exists.

Content of the Notice

Just as the form of notice has become recognized as needing to be written, the content of the notice should state the following:

- the intent to expel the student
- the specific charges against the student
- what rule was broken
- nature of the evidence supporting the charges
- date, time and place where a hearing on the expulsion will commence
- a copy of the procedures that will be followed at the hearing
- a reminder of the rights the student and parents have, including the right to counsel, presentation of witnesses, cross-examination of hostile witnesses, and a copy of the hearing transcript

The language stating that the board has the intent to expel ithe student is necessary. Even if the student has admitted to having broken a rule and no facts are in dispute, the student should not be expelled until there is a hearing. If this were not so, it would be, in effect, a finding of guilt and punishment without a trial.

The statement of charges and evidence must be specific enough to give the student and parents an opportunity to know how to prepare a defense. The degree of specificity required to communicate the necessary content has been subject to court challenge. The courts have given wide latitude to school districts when considering whether the level of specificity was sufficient to provide notice. The *Goss* decision contains clear authority for school authorities to be upheld in their notice practices even though the content of the notice might have been more specific. For example, a Florida court ruled for the school district even though the suspension notice lacked specificity. The notice of the suspension hearing informed the student that she was being charged with "distribution" of marijuana. However, at the hearing she was prosecuted for "possession" of marijuana. The distribution and the possession activities were all part of the same event. The court concluded that the student was put on notice when it was clear what "event" the school was considering. The distribution versus possession distinction is misplaced hairsplitting for a suspension proceeding which is administrative and not criminal in nature. The court noted that the student's argument may have had merit if "she had been accused and tried for ... marijuana but suspended for absenteeism or cheating on an exam."[10] The court relied on *Goss* when it said that: "[I]nterpretation and application of due process are intensely practical matters which negate any concept of inflexible procedures universally applicable to every imaginable situation."[11]

In *Stratton v. Wenona Community Unit District No. 1*, the expulsion notice was challenged for lack of specific content. A male high school student had been involved in a series of altercations across a span of several months. After several of the incidents had occurred, the student was suspended for four days. The notice of that suspension stating the grounds was not in question. However, the decision to proceed to an expulsion came after the superintendent evaluated the totality of the student's behavior following yet another altercation. The notice which was in dispute indicated that the student was being considered for expulsion "for gross misconduct, disobedience, and disrespect." It substantially tracked the language of the Illinois statute which notes the grounds for expulsion. Prior to the decision to recommend the student for expulsion, school officials met with the student's parents and brought them up to date on the most recent acts of misconduct. The parents knew from the meeting that the upcoming expulsion hearing was a culmination of a pattern of misbehavior rather than

---

[10] Student Alpha ID Number Guja v. School Board of Volusa County, 616 So.2d 1011, 1013 (Fla. 1993).
[11] Goss, 419 U.S. at 583.

a punishment for any particular incident. According to the court, "[The] misconduct had simply reached a point where school officials considered him unmanageable... so that references in the notice to specific incidents or definitional rules of the school authority were unnecessary."[12]

It is clear that school authorities must pursue the provision of sufficient content in the notice of expulsion "as a goal." Hair-splitting omissions that may technically offer an argument would, in addition, need to have been the proximate cause in providing a genuine surprise to the student. Where school authorities can show that the student was *constructively* notified by the totality of the disciplinary circumstance, procedural due process can be satisfied. Once again citing the *Stratton* decision: "Due process does not require useless formality in the giving of notice."[13]

Timeliness of the Hearing

That the student must be given notice in sufficient time to prepare a defense has been established since the early 1970s. Exactly how much time must be given is not fixed, although most state statutes allow for at least a week. Where the statute is silent, it is common for the state board of education to provide guidelines.

The Supreme Court of Illinois ruled that two days' notice was sufficient time to prepare for a defense for an expulsion hearing. However, the facts of the case for that ruling showed that parents and student were aware of the instances of misconduct leading up to the expulsion consideration.[14]

In insuring due process, too much time can be as problematic as not enough time. Ideally, school officials should not postpone the hearing any longer than is needed for a defense to be prepared.

In *Garcia v. Los Angeles County Board of Education*,[15] a California appeals court invalidated the expulsion of a junior high school student because the board was not timely in scheduling the hearing. The board conducted the hearing 40 days after the student was removed from school.

---

[12] 133 Ill.2d 413, 435 (1990).
[13] *Id.*
[14] *Id.* at 433.
[15] 177 Cal. Rptr. 29 (Cal.Ct. App. 1981).

Persons to Receive Notice

Unlike suspension notices, in which parent notification is sometimes optional, expulsion notices require that parents and the student be notified. In fact, parents are more often mentioned in state statutes as the recipient of the notice. Most often the student's notice comes in the form of an oral presentation by school officials with a reminder that the parents are going to be sent the written notice.

Sending a written notice to the student can be important when the student has reached the age of 18. The Illinois Association of School Boards recommends that "a copy should be sent to the student who is no longer a minor to avoid a student claim of parental conflict of interest."[16]

Location of Student Pending the Hearing

Where is the student pending the expulsion hearing? Because the student can not be found guilty until the hearing, can the school authorities keep the student out of school until the date? A simple answer is "yes."

As long as the school district moves in a timely manner, the student can remain "out of school" pending the hearing. Having the student remain out of school can be important in maintaining school safety. If the student's offense could represent a danger to the student body, it would be prudent for school authorities to exercise the option of keeping the student out of school. Of course, this is an option to be exercised by school authorities. Some offenses, while warranting expulsion, may not be dangerous behaviors. For example, if a student was caught cheating on a national examination, the school rules may call for consideration for expulsion. However, if the student were to remain in school pending the hearing, the student's prescence would likely not pose a threat to the school environment. Typically, it is the parents of the student who request that the student remain in school.

Must school authorities suspend the student short-term pending the expulsion hearing? This would be unnecessary. However, due to the nature of removing students from school, it is not un-

---

[16] G. Cartwright & A. Schwartz, The School Official's Guide to Student Disciplinary Hearings 19 (1986).

common for the administration to decide to consider expelling a student while the student is out of school serving a short-term suspension or on an emergency suspension. If the student is out because of misbehavior that was an immediate threat to himself or to others, he is on an emergency suspension. The *Goss* Court required that the student be given a hearing as soon as practicable when one could not be given because of the emergency situation.[17] However, if the emergency situation was serious enough for expulsion to be considered, then obviously the student is out of school pending the expulsion hearing. It would be a mutation of the school disciplinary system to recall the student to suspend the student short-term for an offense that calls for a long-term suspension.

A more complicated situation arises when the administration decides to consider an expulsion while a student is out on a short-term suspension. A good example is provided with the *Hill* decision. A Mississippi high school student was involved in two altercations on the same day. The first altercation involved an attack on another student. The consequence was a three-day suspension which was to commence the following day. Later that same day, however, the student was involved in an act of gross insubordination with a member of the school staff. Before the end of the school day, the student was given a five-day suspension for the insubordination. Therefore, the student was to serve a total of eight days of suspension for the two separate instances. Upon return to school on the ninth day, the parents and student were informed that he must remain out of school because the administration had decided to recommend expulsion. The hearing was held approximately two months after the notification of the intent to expel. The excessive length of time between notification and the hearing was not at issue. However, the absence of a separate due process hearing for the removal prior to the hearing was. Specifically, the student challenged the two months of not being able to attend classes pending the expulsion hearing as a deprivation sufficient to have warranted a hearing. The federal court rejected that challenge. It noted that even if the expulsion hearing had been held immediately after the student's return from short-term suspension, it would have resulted in the student being out of school on an expulsion for that same period.[18]

---

[17] Goss, 419 U.S. at 582-583.

[18] Hill v. Rankin County Sch. Dist., 843 F. Supp. 1112 (S.D. Miss. 1993).

The question of "credit for time served pending hearing" has appeared in the case law. To clarify, are school authorities required to "deduct" from the number of days of expulsion to be served those days in which the student was out of school pending the hearing? The answer so far has been "no." The days out of school pending the hearing are simply lost for the student. The current authority coming from the United States Court of Appeals for the Second Circuit would conclude that the process of waiting for the hearing is part of the punishment.[19]

The Formal Hearing

The expulsion hearing has been recognized as basic to the provision of due process since the 1960s The hearing must come *before* the student is formally sentenced. However, the student is usually out of school while waiting for the hearing to be scheduled. As noted earlier, the time that elapses from the student's removal from school and the hearing date is typically added to the sentence.

The conduct of the formal hearing need not meet the standards of a courtroom trial. However, most state statutes provide that the student and parents have such rights as the presentation of witnesses, the student being able to testify in his/her own defense, representation by an attorney, cross-examination of hostile witnesses, and a copy of the record of the proceedings. As long as the formal hearing is conducted in good faith and there are no gross deprivations of rights, the courts are disposed to sustain the actions of school authorities.

Impartial Trier of Fact

The right to a hearing assumes that the school representatives hearing the case will be impartial. To satisfy this requirement, expulsion and long-term suspension hearings are generally conducted by the superintendent or a committee of persons appointed by the board of education. If an appeal is requested by the student or the student's parents, only then does the full board convene.[20]

---

[19] Rosa R. v. Connelly, 889 F.2d 435 (2d Cir. 1989).

[20] *See, e.g.*, Kansas Stat. Ann. § 72-8900 (1997).

For purposes of a fair hearing, impartiality means more than the hearing officials "having nothing against the student." To be impartial means that there is little or no "commingling of the prosecutorial and adjudicatory functions."

In every legal situation where a person's life, liberty or property is at stake, someone acts as the prosecutor on behalf of some authority. The prosecutor is the one who makes the charges, collects the evidence and brings the matter to the attention of someone else — the adjudicator. The one who prosecutes should not be the same as the one who judges.

If the principal acts as the hearing officer for the expulsion, does it provide a prima facie case for an unfair proceeding? No. It is likely that before a court will invalidate an expulsion hearing, it will have to be shown that the principal's involvement has prejudiced the impartiality and fairness which must exist in considering the evidence.

To be absolutely clear, it is not the "intent" or what is in the heart and mind of the hearing officer that contaminates impartiality. It is "prior involvement" with the case of sufficient *degree* and *kind* that would act as a disqualifier.

The federal district court for the Central District of California perhaps put it best when parents of an expelled student challenged the fairness of the hearing that was provided: "The question before the Court is not whether the Board was actually biased, but whether, under the circumstances, there existed probability that the decision maker would be tempted to decide the issues with partiality to one party or the other."[21]

More recently, in *Snyder v. Farnsworth*, a New York federal court considered the question of bias when it was discovered that the impartial trier was related to the school board attorney.[22] The case dealt with three high school students alleged to have brought a hand gun onto school premises in violation of school policy. The infraction called for a long-term suspension. The hearing officer for the formal hearing was Steven Buchyn, an attorney. Mr. Steven Buchyn was the son and law partner of Joseph Buchyn, the board's attorney.

The parents of one of the three students argued that Steven Buchyn could not possibly be impartial because of his relation-

---

[21] Gonzales v. McEuen, 435 F. Supp. 460, 464 (C.D. Cal. 1977).

[22] 896 F. Supp. 96 (N.D.N.Y.1995).

ship to the board attorney. The court found no due process violation because of the relationship. It noted:

> Plaintiffs fail...to make specific allegations concerning any facts of which the hearing officer was made aware concerning the case, or any showing of bias or personal interest in the case which directly impacted upon the outcome of the proceedings. Absent such a showing, the type of relationship alleged by plaintiffs is insufficient to constitute a violation of due process.[23]

The suggestion of *Snyder* is that it may not be enough just to point to commingling, there must be some evidence of contamination of results. Of course, if showing of personal interest could be made, it may be difficult for the school district to defend in the face of obvious commingling. School authorities may be wiser to insure against begging that kind of issue by checking on the possibility of commingling before the hearing proceeds.

In another case, an eleventh grade student was expelled for stealing a school computer. At the formal hearing, the superintendent of schools was present for all the deliberations before the board of education. The board acted as the impartial trier of fact. The parents of the student challenged the decision, arguing that the presence of the superintendent was prejudicial to the board's decision. While the Pennsylvania trial court agreed with the parents, the decision was reversed on appeal. The court of appeals noted that, "...[A] court is bound to affirm the local agency adjudication unless there has been a violation of constitutional rights, an error of law, a violation of agency procedure, or a lack of substantial evidence to support key findings of fact."[24]

Separate Hearings for Multiple Offenders

Another interesting argument coming out of *Snyder* centered on the school district having conducted separate hearings for each of the three students. The issue was that the trier of fact could not have been impartial because the same person presided over all three hearings. Therefore, the finder of fact heard evidence out-

---

[23] *Id.* at 98.

[24] Kish v. Annville-Cleona Sch. Dist., 645 A.2d 361, 362 (1994).

side of the plaintiffs' presence and outside the presence of their counsel that was considered in making the decision to suspend. The court noted that separate hearings do not in themselves violate due process rights. The students did not show that the hearing officer actually considered information that was improper. Therefore, because it could not be demonstrated that any actual prejudice resulted from separate hearings, the argument was rejected.

In the last ten years, court decision have shown that commingly prosecutorial and adjudicatory functions in the formal hearing process does not seem as important as it once did. Certainly, this is one less legal hurdle about which the school must worry. It seems that as long as the complaining party can not show how the commingling resulted in an improper decision, it will not be a problem. The primary upshot of this turn in court thinking is that school authorities are able to take back some of the authority they lost during the previous two decades and able to once again discipline student s as they see fit.

Waiving Hearing Rights

In order for a student to waive the expulsion hearing, it would require "an intentional relinquishment or abandonment of a known right or privilege."[25] In an early case, a Massachusetts federal district court found that a high school student had effectively waived his hearing rights when his father refused to appear at the superintendent's office.[26] However, one year later a contrary ruling was handed down in New York. The principal of a senior high school suspended a 17-year-old for five days. A notice was sent home explaining the reasons for the immediate suspension and that the principal was going to recommend a permanent expulsion to the superintendent. The notice also read: "...[I]f you wish to appeal this suspension, please contact the Superintendent of Schools within five days to arrange a hearing. Unless we hear from you during this period, we will assume that Carmen is to be dropped from our attendance rolls."[27]

---

[25] Johnson v. Zerbst, 304 U.S. 458, 464 (1938).
[26] Grayson v. Malone, 311 F. Supp. 987 (D. Mass. 1970).
[27] MacDonald v. Tompkins, 323 N.Y.S.2d 1002,1003 (Sup. Ct. 1971).

No response came from the MacDonald household. Therefore, the expulsion continued for the remainder of the school year. The MacDonald's sued the school district, claiming a denial of due process since there was no hearing. The school district argued that since there was no request for a hearing, the student "waived his rights."

The court held for the student and reasoned that the school should have scheduled a hearing regardless of the apparent lack of interest from the parents. The district should not have assumed that because there was no communication from the MacDonalds that they had waived their rights.

More recently, in *Coplin v. Conejo Valley Unified School District,*[28] a high school male student claimed he did not receive due process when he was expelled for sexually harassing female students. One of the arguments was that the student was expelled without a hearing. The school district maintained that the student waived his hearing rights because his parents signed a consent form, which effectively waived the hearing. The parents argued they were coerced into signing the form. The court examined the facts surrounding the signing of the form as well as the language of the form itself. In rejecting the parents' argument, the court noted that the form was clear about what would happen if they signed the form. In addition, the parents had received legal advice prior to the signing. Given this evidence, the court concluded that parents had waived the right to a hearing and that no coercion could be found.[29]

Self-Incrimination and the Right to Remain Silent

A related question of whether the student may exercise the "right to remain silent" without penalty has been the subject of court debate. The Fifth Amendment of the U.S. Constitution guarantees in part that "No person ... shall be compelled in any criminal case to be a witness against himself...." Remaining silent is the way in which an accused person will keep from

---

[28] 903 F. Supp, 1377 (C.D. Cal 1995).

[29] *Id.* at 1384.

unwittingly helping the prosecution. The privilege against self-incrimination was clarified in the landmark case *Miranda v. Arizona.*[30]

Anyone being questioned while in official custody related to a criminal investigation, must be advised of their right to remain silent, that any statement made may be used against them, and that they have the right of legal counsel. Not only does a person being detained have the right to remain silent, but also the right to be reminded of this right. While related, they are two distinct rights. The *Miranda* decision is not so much about the privilege of remaining silent as it is about the authorities being required to remind the persons that they indeed have that right. People have exercised their right to remain silent long before *Miranda*. Prior to *Miranda*, however, not everyone being detained knew or remembered that they had a Fifth Amendment protection.

Miranda Warnings for Students

The Miranda question as it relates to student expulsion is "Does a student have a right to remain silent?" If so, under what circumstances? Beyond this question, do school authorities have the legal obligation to provide a Miranda warning before questioning a student? The second question is easier to answer since the law is more settled on the issue.

In a Florida case, a high school student was suspended for smoking marijuana on school grounds. The facts show that the student had been questioned in the school office by the assistant principal as part of the evidence gathering. However, a sheriff's deputy was present. In fact, the deputy admitted to having asked two questions himself during the interrogation.

The parents sued, claiming that the student's suspension was unlawful because no Miranda warning was given to the student prior to the interrogation. It was argued that their son had a right to be Mirandized because a law enforcement officer was present and participated in the interrogation.

The court stated that if a person is taken into custody and questioned by law enforcement officers, then the person must be read

---

[30] 377 U.S. 201 (1966).

his/her Miranda rights. However, a student interrogated by school officials does not have the right to Miranda. Said the court, "It was simply the job of the assistant principal to investigate complaints originating out of activities of students on school grounds. As such, he was a school official not a police official. Therefore, the necessity of Miranda warnings did not exist."[31]

The court did not believe the situation changed because a sheriff's deputy was present. Citing to a South Carolina case, the court noted, "[I]f the policeman stands mute and does not participate, his mere presence does not render it a custodial interrogation."[32]

Student's Right to Remain Silent

In the *Coplin* case discussed earlier, the student claimed he was denied due process on several grounds. One such argument was that he was not told that he had a right to remain silent. However, the court rejected the notion that students had a right to remain silent as part of the suspension process. The court relied on *Goss v. Lopez* for precedent and noted Coplin had no case since "Goss made no mention that [students' had the right to remain silent."[33]

While students may not have a right to remain silent, they nevertheless may still remain silent during questioning. The student may have heard something about the Fifth Amendment and decide it will help if silence is maintained. It is possible that a student may be frightened or confused and therefore rendered speechless. Can school authorities take a student's silence as an admission of guilt? Do students have a right to remain silent under certain circumstances? While there is case law showing that some courts have been willing to grant this right, most have not. However, legal commentators and at least one school board association suggest that students should be allowed to remain silent under special circumstances. Where granting the Fifth Amendment right has been seriously considered, it has been due to a student's being charged with both a school offense and a criminal law violation. The student's argument would be that they cannot be compelled to testify in the disciplinary hearing

---

[31] In the Interest of J.C., 591 So. 2d 315 (Fla. Dist.Ct.App 1991).

[32] *Id.* at 316, citing *In re* Drolshagen, 310 S.E. 2d 927 (S.C. 1984).

[33] Coplin, 903 F.Supp. at 1387.

because the testimony might later be used against them in the criminal proceeding (it being safe to assume that the school is able to schedule a hearing well before a case can rise to the top of a typically crowded juvenile court docket). In rejecting this line of argument, the courts have held that students could object at the criminal trial to incriminating statements made at the expulsion hearing. Indeed using this procedural approach instead of invoking the Fifth Amendment has been the dominant position of the courts.[34] Wright has maintained that students cannot be compelled to testify against themselves at a school hearing when there are pending criminal charges for the same conduct. Further, the student should be able to exercise the right to remain silent without fear of reprisal from school authorities.[35]

The Illinois Association of School Boards (IASB) has pointed out that because school boards do not have the power of subpoena, they cannot require students to attend even their own hearing, let alone require them to testify. The IASB recommends that if the charges at the hearing may become an issue before a criminal court, the right of the student to invoke the Fifth Amendment should be respected. It further recommends that no adverse inference should be drawn against the student who elects to remain silent. Consistent with most case law, the IASB does suggest that boards discover whether the student is going to be able to suppress the hearing testimony at the later court proceeding. If it can be done, then a board may safely insist on the student's testimony at the hearing.[36]

Double Jeopardy

In addition to the right to remain silent, the Fifth Amendment is also the source of a citizen's protection against double jeopardy. The Amendment says in part "... nor shall any person be subject to the same offense to be twice put in jeopardy of life or limb." No court has been willing to extend the double jeopardy protection to students. The double jeopardy protection is meant for those who have criminal charges against them. The individual may not be tried twice for the same criminal offense.

---

[34] *See* Johnson v. Board of Educ., 310 N.Y.S. 2d 429 (Sup.Ct. 1970).

[35] C. Wright, *The Constitution on the Campus,* 5 Vand. L. Rev. 1027 (1969).

[36] C. Cartwright & A. Schwartz, The School Official's Guide to Student Disciplinary Hearings 45-46 (1986).

However, if a person is tried for the criminal offense of battery, the citizen who was battered by the accused is perfectly free to sue for damages. The liability suit is a matter of civil law for which double jeopardy does not apply.[37] A criminal proceeding followed by a civil proceeding or vice versa, is not an offense to double jeopardy even though the same conduct is at issue.

Since school disciplinary hearings are not criminal proceedings, double jeopardy would not apply. Therefore, school authorities would not be required to postpone an expulsion hearing waiting for the outcome of criminal charges. The school could expel a student for misconduct even though the student was found "not guilty" by a court. A disciplinary panel does not have the same burden of proof as a criminal court. School authorities need only establish the veracity of the charge by believable evidence. A criminal court must see that guilt has been established "beyond a reasonable doubt."

Likewise, school authorities may punish a student twice for the same offense. An Ohio appellate court let stand the expulsion of a student by the superintendent following the return of the student after a ten-day suspension by the principal.

The student was expelled for the same incident which resulted in the suspension. The court considered the suspension and the expulsion two separate kinds of punishment. A suspension is a punishment imposed because of the immediate nature of the offense and is within the scope of the principal's authority. The expulsion is a more considered punishment that may be imposed by the superintendent after a thorough review.[38]

Public Hearing

Does the student have the right to an expulsion hearing held in public? Much depends on the statues in a particular state. Most states have Open Meeting Acts or "sunshine laws" that guide the meetings of all public bodies. Often school disciplinary proceedings are exempt from the Open Meeting Act. In order to be clear, it is necessary to distinguish between deliberations in public and decisions in public. When the Open Meetings Act exempts school disciplinary proceedings, it is exempting the deliberations,

---

[37] Dunn v. California Dept. of Corrections, 401 F.2d 340 (9th Cir. 1968); Filmon Process Corp. v. Spell-Right Corp., 404 F.2d 1351 (D.C. Cir. 1968).

[38] Fleetwood v. Board of Educ., 252 N.E.2d 318 (Ohio 1969).

not the decision, from the public. Therefore, if the state statute exempts disciplinary hearings, while the board can go into "executive" session (behind closed doors), it must come out into an open meeting for the actual decision. The decision is often by roll call vote. So, the entitlement to an open hearing is an entitlement for the accused to present his case in public, not to hear arguments with the deliberations of the trier.

In a Texas case, a high school student objected to the executive session to which the board adjourned after it heard testimony in a public hearing. The Texas appeals court rejected the argument, finding no violation of the Open Meetings Act.[39] In this case, the board president asked whether there were any objections to the board going into executive session. The student raised no objections.

There is a question whether the student can override the board's decision to go into executive session. In other words, if the Open Meeting Act provides for an exception, who exercises that option? The answer seems to be that the decision is in the hands of the governmental body. Therefore, the student could not override the board. While hard to find, a state statute could provide that the student has the right to override an executive session decision. If the student will have that right it is likely to be provided for in the local board policy.

In considering some of these issues, the Ohio Court of Appeals rejected a student's claim for violation of the Open Meetings Act.

The student claimed that the Ohio Open Meetings Act "required" that a board of education may not go into executive session for disciplinary deliberations unless requested to do so by the student. The court noted the statute did provide for a student to decide on whether the student had a public hearing, but that did not preclude the board from doing any deliberating in executive session.[40]

An alternative to the all-public or all-closed hearing is a combination of both. The expulsion hearing itself, where the charges are read and witnesses are presented, might be closed. The meeting where the board hands down its decision could be open to the public. In this way, the student would be protected from the public knowing all of the details, while the public would have the privilege of being present for the actual decision.

---

[39] United Indep. Sch. Dist. v. Gonzalez, 911 S.W.2d 118 (Tex. 1995).

[40] Armstead v. Lima City Bd. of Educ., 600 N.E.2d 1085 (Ohio 1991).

Right to Counsel

The right to counsel is not fundamental to providing due process. Much depends on the extent of the deprivation that is at stake. If the deprivation is high, the courts will likely require that the accused be represented by counsel. In the *Goss* case, the Court was not willing to require that counsel represent a student for suspensions of ten days or less. However, the Court specifically recognized the student's right to counsel in "more difficult cases" when it stated that "Longer suspensions or expulsions for the remainder of the school term, or permanently, may require more formal procedures."[41]

Today most state statutes provide the right to counsel for an expulsion. Whether a statute provides the right to counsel or not does not affect the student's right to have representation by parents. The student's right to be represented by parents is also extended to another adult if the parents are deceased, are unavailable, or are incapacitated or unable to properly assist the student.

If the school board attorney were to be present at a hearing, even for a short-term suspension, the student could not be denied the right to also have an attorney present. If this were not the case, the hearing would be unfair to the student.

In the *Coplin* case cited earlier, the student argued a number of due process issues. One issue was that he should have been informed of his right to counsel at the initial short-term suspension hearing. This was argued because the short-term suspension became a long-term suspension while the student was serving out his first suspension. The court rejected this notion. It reasoned that no right to be informed of the representation of counsel exists for a short-term suspension. The *Goss* decision contemplated no such right.[42]

On the issue of attorney's fees, thus far the courts have not extended free legal counsel for the regular education student.

---

[41] Goss, 419 U.S. at 584.

[42] Coplin, 903 F. Supp. at 1388.

Evidence

As mentioned earlier, expulsion hearings are administrative proceedings not criminal trials. Therefore, the technical rules of evidence do not apply. The courts have consistently declined to impose the formal procedures and rules of evidence which govern court trials on student disciplinary proceedings.

While expulsion panels may not have to follow strict rules of evidence, this does not mean they may ignore the basic standards of fairness. For example, school authorities must give students access to the evidence the board intends to use to make its case. The board must have some notion of what can be recognized as sufficient evidence. While some hearsay can be admitted, the student should not be found guilty solely on basis of hearsay.

Access to Evidence

Due process requires that the accused be informed as to what evidence the authorities may use. The concept has been applied to school disciplinary proceedings for quite some time.

In Batavia, Ohio, a 16-year-old student had been charged with the possession and attempted sale of marijuana. An expulsion hearing was conducted by the principal and superintendent. In the process, a juvenile court officer testified that there was no need for the student to undergo drug counseling. The officer recommended that the boy be immediately returned to school. However, the principal and superintendent offered to expunge the records only if the parents would agree to a transfer the boy to a vocational school. The parents declined the offer. They were then informed that their son was expelled for the remainder of the fall semester. The parents appealed the decision to the school board.

Ten days later, the board met in executive session to consider the expulsion appeal. After hearing arguments, the board met in private with the principal and superintendent to review the evidence. It was during the private session with the board that the superintendent revealed new evidence and told the board that the student had confessed to a counselor with the county alchoholism clinic.

The superintendent had this information before the appeal hearing but wanted to apprise the board so the student could not rebut at the open hearing. When the board decided to uphold the expulsion, the student filed suit in federal court.

It was argued that the student was denied procedural due process when the superintendent disclosed to the board, during their closed deliberations, new evidence which had not been presented during the open hearing. A unanimous court held for the student. It opined that while this was an expulsion case, the minimum requirements even for a short-term suspension had not been met.

Regarding the behavior of the superintendent, the court concluded: "Such a tactic completely deprived Newsome [the student] of any opportunity to rebut the evidence and amounted to a clear deprivation of his right to procedural due process of law."[43]

Sufficiency of Evidence

A school cannot expel a student without enough evidence to prove the charges that have been made. In other words, the charges must be supported by substantial evidence.

Substantial evidence has been defined by the U.S. Supreme Court as: "[S]ubstantial evidence is more than a mere scintilla. It means such relevant evidence as a reasonable mind might accept as adequate to support a conclusion...."[44]

Deciding what is substantial evidence, however, isn't always a simple matter. For example, in one such case, the board expelled a student after hearing conflicting testimony from the defending student and a second student. Although it was essentially a classic your-word-against-mine scenario, the board concluded the second student's story was more credible. The expelled student appealed, claiming there was not enought evidence to warrant his expulsion. In handling the appeal, the Pennsylvania court recognized that the board did not have "clear and convincing evidence," nor did it even constitute a "preponderance of evidence." Nevertheless, the court found the evidence — the second student's testimony — was substantial. Therefore, the decision of the board was upheld.[45] This case stands for the proposition that

---

[43] Newsome v. Batavia Local School District, 842 F.2d 920, 928 (6th Cir. 1988).

[44] Universal Camera Corp. v. NLRB, 340 U.S. 474, 621 (1951).

[45] Kish, 645 A.2d at 342.

the substantial evidence standard is not difficult for school boards to meet. The technical rules of evidence will not rule out a decision that a board makes on *any* evidence that in its view is enough to convince them. The courts continue to give great deference to school board decision making. Courts are reluctant to substitute their discretion on school matters for that of the school board.

Another case in Florida demonstrates the Court's deference to the authority of school boards to determine sufficiency of evidence. A high school student was expelled for selling "speed." The expulsion was challenged for lack of sufficient evidence. Later it was found that the pills the student was selling were actually caffeine, which is not an illegal drug. However, the court held that, "[A]lthough the pills sold by appellant were later shown to be caffeine, there is evidence, which the Board was free to believe, that appellant represented the pills as 'speed.'"[46] Thus the student's expulsion was upheld.

However, in a case with similar facts, the expulsions were reversed by the court for lack of evidence. Here, a student go-between was asked to buy "caffeine" pills. Neither the seller nor the students for whom the sale was made ever represented the pills as "speed" even though the go-between purchaser "thought" they were speed.

Exclusionary Rule

From earlier discussions, it was learned that Miranda warnings in school disciplinary proceedings do not apply. In the law, the remedy for not having provided the Miranda warning is the exclusionary rule. It means that illegally obtained evidence will be excluded from consideration at the trial. The exclusionary rule was intended to be the citizen's protection from overly zealous police officers' obtaining evidence by illegal means. e.g., no search warrant or forcing a confession.

A good application of this standard to the school setting was seen in the *Birdsey*. In *Birdsey,* a high school student was expelled for selling drugs. The trial court had excluded statements made by the student during his initial questioning on the grounds that school authorities had not "Mirandized" the student. The Michigan Appellate Court reversed. It pointed out that the

---

[46] Jones v. Brevard County School Board, 470 So. 2d 760 (Fla. Dist. Ct. App. 1985).

trial court erred in excluding the statements of the student, "[S]tatements taken without benefit of Miranda warnings are not barred from evidence in a civil proceeding... Inasmuch that the evidentiary hearing conducted in this case was civil and not criminal the trial court erred in excluding plaintiff's written statement on *Miranda* grounds."[47]

Because *Miranda* does not apply in school disciplinary proceedings, the exclusionary rule will not apply.

Voluntary Confessions

The courts have said that the test for the voluntary nature of a confession is if the defendant's will to resist was so overborne as to bring about a confession not freely self-determined.[48]

However, in the school setting, can a student ever be free enough to provide a voluntary confession? Is not the subordinate position of a student, coupled with his/her immaturity, lack of knowledge and confidence so pronounced that it can be argued whether a student could ever "voluntarily" confess?

The question has surfaced in the related area of search and seizure in the public schools. It has been noted that federal courts have rejected the argument that students can give consent to be searched. The reasoning is that students in school are afraid not to cooperate with school authorities. Therefore, consent cannot be freely given.[49]

Hearsay

Hearsay may be admitted in school disciplinary proceedings. In fact, it has been recommended that hearing panels be liberal in allowing evidence and not disallow testimony because it is hearsay. There have been circumstances when hearsay alone has constituted substantial evidence. The Fifth Circuit Court of Appeals has noted several instances when hearsay can be admit-

---

[47] Birdsey v. Grand Blanc Comm. Sch., 344 N.W. 2d at 344.

[48] Rogers v. Richmond, 365 U.S. 534, 544 (1961).

[49] L. Rossow and J. Stefkovich, Search and Seizure in the Public Schools, 2d ed., 43 (NOLPE Monograph 1995).

ted because the circumstances support the probative value of the evidence. Those instances might be when:

- direct evidence is unavailable
- the hearsay evidence is unchallenged
- the statements are made by outside persons, but they have no bias and no interest in the outcome of the hearing.[50]

Imposing Penalties

An Indiana case considered whether school authorities have any obligation to consider "other factors" surrounding the character of the accused student in deciding on the punishment. In other words, do school officials have to follow some form of sentencing guidelines?

The accused student admitted to using marijuana while on school grounds. He was subsequently expelled. The proceeding was later challenged because the board had not taken the student's "good standing" into account when deliberating over the expulsion. The student argued that the board's decision to expel him was flawed because it was only based on whether he did or did not smoke the marijuana. It was further argued that the board should have considered his previous disciplinary record (which showed no prior disciplinary incident), his academic standing, his numerous contributions to the school and the fact that there was little evidence of a recurring problem. Rejecting the student's argument, the court opined:

> If plaintiff were to prevail in this action, it would mean that school boards would have to apply two different standards when considering the exclusion of students for the use of marijuana. One standard would apply to the "good student" who, under plaintiff's theory, should not be expelled because he is a "good student." Since such alleged "mitigating circumstances" are not present in the case of a "bad" student," it logically follows from the plaintiff's argument that such a "bad student" should be expelled.[51]

---

[50] School Board v. H.E.W., 525 F. 2d 900, 906 (5th Cir. 1976).

[51] Forrest v. School City of Hobart, 498 N.E. 2d 14,18 (Ind. Ct. App. 1986).

Finally, the court pointed out that "Even if we were to adopt Forrest's characterization of his "good standing" in school, we disagree that the school was required to consider these factors."[52]

Witnesses

Basic to due process is the right of the accused to confront and cross-examine witnesses as well as present witnesses on their own behalf. This right is a large part of presenting evidence. In many cases, the witnesses' testimony is the primary evidence. The witness right was applied to the school setting as far back as the turn of the century. In recognizing the right of the student to present, confront and cross-examine witnesses, a Massachusetts court said: "The hearing afforded may be of no value if relevant evidence, when offered, is refused admission, or those who otherwise would testify in behalf of the excluded pupil are prevented by action of the school."[53] In the landmark *Goss v. Lopez* decision the Court did suggest that expulsions might include more formal procedures such as the student's right to cross-examine and present witnesses.[54] However, this right is not absolute.

In one case, one of the issues before the federal court was whether the student to be expelled had a right to confront his accusers. The student was accused of sexually harassing female classmates. In this case, the court was concerned that if the school was forced to identify the student accusers, it would deter other students from coming forward in the future. In addition, student victims have an interest in not being identified because of the possibility of experiencing continued harassment. While this case deals with sexual harassment, the fear of retribution is what this factor turns on. Therefore analogous consideration would apply to the full range of disciplinary activities. Peer considerations of retribution could apply to any "ratting" on a fellow student. The court needs to determine whether the retribution is real. Also, it is important to note that considerations of loss of reputation, in other words, being known as a squealer, is not the same as fear of retribution. It is not likely the court would set aside the confrontation principle to maintain a student's status among peers.[55]

---

[52] *Id.* at 17.
[53] Morrison v. City of Lawrence, 186 Mass. 456, 460 (1904).
[54] Goss, 419 U.S. at 584.
[55] Coplin, 903 F.Supp. at 1383.

Recording the Hearing

Stenographic or mechanical recordings of the expulsion hearing may be required by state statute. Where required, the hearing panel will be expected to follow the statute without exception. The *Coplin* case also raised, as one of many due process issues questioned, the issue of a record of the hearing, or lack thereof. The State of California has no record keeping requirement for expulsion hearings. Nevertheless, it was argued that keeping a record of the hearing is a requirement under the Due Process Clause.

The court rejected the due process argument. It noted that anywhere in the hearing process a competent attorney could construct a record. For example, if student witnesses were called by the student but were barred from testifying, deposing the student witnesses to tell what happened to them as they appeared to testify is an available record. Also, correspondence between the attorney for the student and school authorities could represent "a record" which might be used for an appeal.[56]

Appeal

Whether a student has the right to appeal an expulsion decision is a matter of state law. The probable routes the appeal might take depend on what level of school officials are involved in the initial decision. When the superintendent or a board committee initially hears the case, the appeal would be to the full board and then to the State Board of Education or a hearing officer representing the State Board. If the full board has made the initial decision, the appeal would be to the State Board.

Where state law differs is on what happens after the administrative appeals have been exhausted. The option of whether the student may appeal to the state court will vary.

In Vermont, a student who wished to appeal a decision of the local board regarding school attendance was denied that opportunity. The decision to deny the appeal was challenged in the State Supreme Court. Finding no fault in the denial, the court held that the legislature provided no right to appeal a decision of the State Board. Since there is no absolute right to appellate

---

[56] *Id.* at 1387.

review of administrative decisions, the decision of the State Board as authorized by statute "shall be final."[57]

Often the state statutes will permit an appeal to the state courts but only after all administrative appeals have been exhausted. In recent years the significance of state statutes permitting appeals to the state courts has been diminished. Because student expulsions concern issues surrounding due process and the 14th Amendment, a federal question may exist. Therefore, student plaintiffs can sue under section 1983 of the Civil Rights Act of 1964. In many instances raising the issue to the level of a constitutional tort has advantages superior to suing in the state courts.

[57] Mason v. Thetford Bd., 457 A. 2d 647, 649 (Vt. 1982).

SHORT-TERM SUSPENSIONS

The law of short-term suspensions (ten days or less) is still governed by the landmark United States Supreme Court decision of *Goss v. Lopez*.[58] The decision grew out of a situation in Ohio that was typical of the way many public schools handled student discipline in the 1970s.

The nine plaintiffs in *Goss* were all students in the Columbus public schools. They were accused of engaging in various types of misbehavior that disrupted the educational environment, including engaging in student demonstrations. Each of the students was suspended for up to ten days, but no student was provided a hearing, either before the suspensions or within a reasonable time thereafter.[59]

At the time, Ohio law gave school principals the power to suspend students for up to ten days without prior notice or hearing. The only procedure required by state statute was that parents had to be notified within 24 hours of the suspension.[60] Thus, the students' suspension in *Goss* was in full accordance with state law.

The suspended students brought suit in federal court, arguing that the state statute was facially invalid because it provided for no procedural due process prior to a suspension. The students sought an order restraining school officials from imposing future suspensions and demanded that the record of their suspensions be removed from the school's files. A three-judge federal district court ruled for the students, holding that they had been denied procedural due process. The court declared the Ohio statute unconstitutional as violative of the Fourteenth Amendment. The Columbus school district appealed to the United States Supreme Court.[61]

The school district made two principal arguments before the Supreme Court. First, it argued that students had no constitutional right to an education, so a suspension from school did not implicate the Fourteenth Amendment. Second, the district argued, even if the Fourteenth Amendment applied, the due process clause protected against only "severe" or "grievous" losses. A ten-day suspension from school, said the district, did not constitute a severe deprivation.[62]

---

58 419 U.S. 565 (1975).

59 *Id.* at 568-71.

60 Ohio Rev. Code Ann. § 3313.66 (1972).

61 419 U.S. at 571-72.

62 *Id.* at 572, 575.

The Court rejected both arguments. As to the first, the Court noted that even though the students may not have had a direct constitutional right to education, they still had protected interests created by state laws obligating the state to provide free public education and requiring compulsory school attendance. Under Ohio law, said the Court, the students "plainly had legitimate claims of entitlement to a public education."[63] In turn, that legitimate entitlement implicated both property and liberty interests protected by the due process clause.[64] Thus, the Constitution demanded that fair procedures be used to determine if misconduct occurred before a student could be suspended.

The Court also rejected the school district's argument that suspensions were not serious enough to implicate the Fourteenth Amendment. To determine whether due process requirements apply, said the Court, "we must look not to the 'weight' but to the *nature* of the interest at stake."[65] Based on the extreme importance of education, suspension for anything more than a "trivial period" would be substantial enough to invoke the protections of the due process clause. In the Court's view, the suspensions at issue in *Goss* were not trivial:

> Appellees were excluded from school only temporarily, it is true, but the length and consequent severity of a deprivation, while another factor to weigh in determining the appropriate form of hearing, "is not decisive of the basic right" to a hearing of some kind. . . . The Court's view has been that as long as property deprivation is not *de minimis,* its gravity is irrelevant to the question whether account must be taken of the Due Process Clause. . . . A ten-day suspension from school is not *de minimis* in our view and may not be imposed in complete disregard of the Due Process Clause.[66]

Once it is determined that the due process clause applies, the next question is what process is due. It is in this area that the Court's guidance has been rather vague. What is required, said the Court, is "*some* kind" of notice and hearing. What that means depends on the circumstances of each case, but at a minimum, a

---

[63] *Id.* at 573.

[64] Students' liberty interests were implicated, said the Court, because even short-term suspensions from school could "seriously damage the students' standing with their fellow pupils and their teachers as well as interfere with later opportunities for higher education and employment." *Id.* at 575.

[65] *Id.* at 575-76 (emphasis in original).

[66] *Id.* at 576 (quoting Fuentes v. Shevin, 407 U.S. 67, 86 (1972)).

student suspended for ten days or less must be afforded: (1) oral or written notice of the charges against the student; (2) the basis of the accusation; and (3) some kind of hearing with the opportunity to present the student's side of the story.[67]

The Court's language suggests that the hearing can be informal. Indeed, the Court indicated that as a general rule, a student in a shortterm suspension hearing has no right to counsel, no right to confront and cross-examine witnesses, and no right to present one's own witnesses. Thus, a school district is *not required* to adhere to these formal procedures, although it may *permit* such formality if it chooses to do so.[68]

The *Goss* Court also stated that notice and a hearing may take place immediately after a student's misconduct. Thus, ordinarily there should be no reason why the notice and hearing do not *precede* the suspension. The Court did recognize, however, that in emergency situations, when a student's presence "poses a continuing danger to persons or property or an ongoing threat of disrupting the academic process," the student "may be immediately removed from school."[69] In such an instance, school officials must be given latitude to deal with the emergency first. As a result, the notice and hearing may take place after the student's effective suspension.

While the *Goss* decision set forth minimum standards for short-term suspensions, it left many questions unanswered. For example, what kind of notice will suffice to meet the Court's "some kind" standard? How informal can the hearing be? Do school officials need to provide procedural due process for students being removed from bus service or extracurricular activities? What process is due a student who is given an in-school suspension? Answers to these and related questions can be gained only by a careful examination of the case law in the last two decades, since *Goss* was decided. The following sections address these issues.

Notice

The Court in *Goss* required only that students facing short-term suspension be given "some kind" of notice of the charges against them. The lower courts have interpreted that standard

---

[67] *Id.* at 579-81.

[68] *Id.* at 583. The Court left open the possibility that more formal procedures might be *required*, even for short-term suspensions, in "unusual situations." *Id.* at 584. It did not elaborate, however, on what might constitute such an unusual situation.

[69] *Id.* at 582.

liberally, deferring to school officials and allowing them flexibility in dealing with student misconduct.

In a recent New York case involving a five-day suspension, the court stated that charges in a student disciplinary proceeding need not be as specific as those required in a criminal proceeding. They should be "sufficiently specific," however, to advise the student of the incidents giving rise to the proceeding.[70]

Substantial compliance appears to be sufficient to overcome technical violations of notice standards. For example, a Florida court held that no due process violation occurred when the school's notice to a student alleged *distribution* of marijuana, even though the student ultimately was suspended for mere *possession* of marijuana.[71] In another case, a federal district court upheld the five-day suspension of a student who violated an obscenity regulation, even though the decision to suspend was made before the student was notified of the reason.[72] The court reasoned that the student had notice in a student handbook that such conduct could result in suspension, school officials told the student of the reason for the suspension later that day, and the student and his mother had an opportunity to argue against the suspension before it actually took effect. Under those circumstances, held the court, due process requirements had been met.[73]

Similarly, a federal judge in *Bystrom v. Fridley High School*[74] forgave a school's violation of a state statute requiring written notice to a student at or before the time suspension takes place. School officials instead mailed written notice to the student's parents on the day of the suspension. That technical violation, said the court, was de minimis.[75] In the same opinion, the court even suggested that use of a pretextual reason for suspension would not constitute a due process violation. The student had distributed an unauthorized newspaper at school. An article in the paper made light of an earlier act of vandalism at the home of a teacher. When the school notified the student's parents that their son was facing suspension for "advocating violence against teachers," the parents argued that that reason was simply a pretext, that the real reason for the discipline was the student's distribution of the pa-

---

[70] Board of Educ. v. Commissioner of Educ., 690 N.E.2d 480, 483 (N.Y. 1997).

[71] Student Alpha Id No. Guja v. School Bd., 616 So. 2d 1011 (Fla. App. 1993).

[72] Heller v. Hodgin, 928 F. Supp. 789 (S.D. Ind. 1996).

[73] *Id.* at 795.

[74] 686 F. Supp. 1387 (D. Minn.), *aff'd*, 855 F.2d 855 (8th Cir. 1988).

[75] *Id.* at 1395 & n.6.

per. The court rejected the parents' pretext argument, stating that in light of overwhelming evidence that some penalty would be imposed, it was irrelevant that the asserted reason in the notice may have been pretextual.[76]

While the parents in *Bystrom* were provided written notice of their son's suspension hearing, there is no constitutional right of parental notice. Unless prescribed by state law or local district policy, parents need not be notified.[77]

Unlike long-term suspensions and expulsions, typically little or no time lapses between the short-term suspension notice and the commencement of an informal hearing. In practice, the student often is called or brought to the school disciplinarian's office, where the student is informed that he or she is about to be suspended. The hearing generally begins after this announcement. Neither students nor their parents are entitled to advance notice for the purpose of more fully preparing for a suspension hearing.[78]

Nor must students be informed of *all* possible charges against them prior to suspension, according to a recent federal court of appeals decision. The Seventh Circuit held that a prehearing notice is not rendered invalid by a post-hearing notification of *additional* charges and reasons for the suspension.[79] The student in the case was informed only of an insubordination charge prior to the hearing, but additional charges of disorderly conduct, possession of a weapon, and gang activity were added to the notice of suspension. In upholding the school's actions, the Seventh Circuit stated that as long as the student is given pre-suspension notice of "at least one proper charge," the later identification of additional charges "is of no consequence."[80]

Another aspect of the notice issue involves notice of the type of misconduct that may subject a student to suspension. A school district may not discipline students for infractions of rules or regulations of which the students were not apprised.[81] This principle led an Ohio court to strike down a five-day suspension for possession of tobacco on the ground that the student code of conduct did not explicitly describe such possession as suspendable conduct.[82]

---

[76] *Id.* at 1394.

[77] Zehner v. Central Berkshire Regional Sch. Dist., 921 F. Supp. 850, 859 (D. Mass 1995).

[78] *Id.* at 861 (rejecting requirement of one to five days' advance notice prior to three-day suspension for use of alcohol at school dance).

[79] Smith v. Severn, 129 F.3d 419 (7th Cir. 1997).

[80] *Id.* at 428.

[81] Martinez v. School Dist. No. 60, 852 P.2d 1275, 1279 (Colo. App. 1992).

[82] Wilson v. South Central Local Sch. Dist., 669 N.E.2d 277 (Ohio App. 1995).

School districts should be clear in spelling out disciplinary regulations to avoid vagueness challenges.[83] Likewise, they would be well advised to include possible penalties for violations. In *Palmer v. Merluzzi*,[84] a student argued that his due process rights were violated because he had not been informed in the notice of charges that he could face athletic as well as academic suspension. The court rejected his argument on the ground that he had constructive notice of the possible sanctions because they had been published in school materials.

Hearing Procedures

Some form of hearing is required prior to any suspension beyond a trivial period.[85] However, the hearing need not be elaborate or formal. All that is required is "an informal give-and-take between the student and disciplinarian."[86] At the heart of this informal hearing is the opportunity for the accused student to explain his or her conduct. As long as students are afforded a reasonable chance to tell their side of the story prior to a suspension, courts are unlikely to find hearings procedurally defective.[87]

The importance of the student's opportunity to explain is illustrated in *Zehner v. Central Berkshire Regional School District*.[88] The student in that case was accused of drinking alcohol at a school dance. The court upheld the student's suspension because he was notified of the charges and afforded a hearing prior to the suspension. Significantly, the court also held that an administrator's

---

[83] *See* Wiemerslage v. Maine Township High Sch. Dist. 207, 29 F.3d 1149 (7th Cir. 1994) ("loitering" provision in disciplinary rule not unconstitutionally vague).

[84] 868 F.2d 90 (3d Cir. 1989).

[85] Goss v. Lopez, 419 U.S. 565, 576 (1975); Rossman v. Conran, 572 N.E.2d 728, 730 (Ohio App. 1988).

[86] Byrd v. Irmo High Sch., 468 S.E.2d 861, 868 (S.C. 1996) (quoting *Goss*, 419 U.S. at 584). *See also* Keough v. Tate County Bd. of Educ., 748 F.2d 1077, 1080 (5th Cir. 1984).

[87] *See, e.g.*, Smith v. Severn, 129 F.3d 419, 428 (7th Cir. 1997) (student afforded due process with notice of violation and opportunity for student and mother to tell their side of story); Donovan v. Ritchie, 68 F.3d 14, 17-18 (1st Cir. 1995) (adequate due process when principal cited various disciplinary regulations and student took advantage of multiple opportunities to explain); Bonner v. Lincoln Parish Sch. Bd., 685 So. 2d 432, 435 (La. App. 1996) (adequate due process when student given notice and several opportunities to explain); Wayne County Bd. of Educ. v. Tyre, 404 S.E.2d 809, 811 (Ga. App. 1991) (adequate due process when student notified of charges and given opportunity to answer).

[88] 921 F. Supp. 850 (D. Mass. 1995).

factual error in the charges was not fatal as long as the student had the opportunity to rebut the administrator's contentions.[89]

Formal rules of evidence do not apply in student suspension hearings. Indeed, all of the evidence presented may be hearsay.[90] Nonetheless, there must be some factual basis to support even a short-term suspension. As one court recently put it, "[t]he decision to suspend a student must be based on competent and substantial evidence that the student actually participated in the conduct charged."[91]

Students facing a short-term suspension are not entitled to adequate time to prepare a defense. Often the "hearing" on a short-term suspension will take place immediately after the student's alleged misconduct. For example, in *Baxter v. Round Lake Area Schools*,[92] the federal district court held there was no due process violation when, following a fight at school, one of the students involved was taken immediately to the dean's ofice and given a chance to tell his side of the story.

The suspension hearing need not be immediate, however, in order to be timely. In many cases, the elapse of a few days for information gathering prior to the hearing will not be unreasonable. In the *Zehner* case, for example, the court approved a Monday suspension hearing following misconduct the previous Friday night.[93] Lengthy delays, however, may not pass muster. In light of the hearing's informality and the lack of any strict evidentiary requirements, little need exists for parties to have extended periods of time in which to build their cases.

No particular form is prescribed for the short-term suspension hearing. In fact, the Eleventh Circuit has upheld a *telephone* hearing which took place a few hours after the incident giving rise to the suspension. The form of the hearing, said the court, was irrelevant because the student and her mother were apprised of the charges and given an opportunity to explain the student's conduct.[94]

School districts certainly may permit more formality, and more process, but it is not required. In *Wiemerslage v. Maine Township High School District 207*,[95] the court considered a three-day sus-

---

[89] *Id.* at 861.
[90] Board of Educ. v. Commissioner of Educ., 690 N.E.2d 480, 484 (N.Y. 1997).
[91] *Id.*
[92] 856 F. Supp. 438 (N.D. Ill. 1994).
[93] 921 F. Supp. at 860.
[94] C.B. *ex rel.* Breeding v. Driscoll, 82 F.3d 383, 386-87 (11th Cir. 1996).
[95] 824 F. Supp. 136 (N.D. Ill. 1993).

pension which followed formal notice, two informal hearings, and one formal hearing at which the student was allowed an attorney. Such formality, concluded the court, far exceeded the process that is due for such a short suspension.[96]

Indeed, even when a suspension would result in the loss of course credit, the courts have been unwilling to require a formal hearing. In *Keough v. Tate County Board of Education*,[97] the student's suspension was imposed during final semester examinations, which effectively meant the student would fail some of his coursework. Nonetheless, the Fifth Circuit found no procedural due process violation because the student was suspended only for ten days and had received both sufficient notice and the opportunity to explain his behavior at an informal "give-and-take session" with the principal.[98]

The *Goss* Court suggested that as a general rule, a student in a short-term suspension hearing has no right to counsel, no right to confront and cross-examine witnesses, and no right to present one's own witnesses.[99] The lower courts have consistently refused to require such rights. Students have no right to cross-examine or even to know the identities of their accusers.[100] Nor do they have a right to counsel or a right to remain silent.[101]

Emergency Suspensions

The *Goss* decision recognized an exception to the general rule that students are entitled to notice and some kind of hearing prior to a short-term suspension. In emergency situations, when a student's presence "poses a continuing danger to persons or property or an ongoing threat of disrupting the academic process," the student may be removed immediately without a hearing.[102] Even in such emergency cases, however, the student must be given a hearing later, when the danger has subsided.

The emergency suspension has been utilized in cases involving students who carry dangerous weapons to school,[103] or students who cause physical harm to others. In one recent case, the Elev-

---

[96] *Id.* at 142.

[97] 748 F.2d 1077 (5th Cir. 1984).

[98] *Id.* at 1080.

[99] *See* 419 U.S. at 583.

[100] Paredes v. Curtis, 864 F.2d 426, 429 (6th Cir. 1988); Coplin v. Conejo Valley Unified Sch. Dist., 903 F. Supp. 1377, 1387 (C.D. Cal. 1995).

[101] *Coplin*, 903 F. Supp. at 1388 (5-day suspension for sexual harassment).

[102] 419 U.S. at 582-83.

[103] *See, e.g.*, McClain v. Lafayette County Bd. of Educ., 673 F.2d 106 (5th Cir. 1982).

enth Circuit upheld the immediate removal of a student, without an opportunity for the student to explain, after she injured the principal during an altercation.[104]

The physical harm rationale also has been invoked in a case involving drug dealing. A student in *Salazar v. Luty*[105] was suspended for two days prior to a hearing for selling drugs. The student argued that the immediate suspension was unlawful because the act of selling marijuana was not intrinsically harmful. The court rejected the student's argument, stating that black market drug dealing was "closely involved with physical harm."[106]

Suspension from Extracurricular Activities

The courts generally have been unsympathetic to due process claims when students are suspended from participation in extracurricular activities. In fact, most courts hold that a student's interest in extracurricular activities is not constitutionally protected at all because no property or liberty interest is implicated.

In *Pegram v. Nelson*,[107] an early case decided four years after *Goss*, a student who stole a wallet at a basketball game received a ten-day academic suspension and a four-month suspension from all extracurricular activities. In upholding both suspensions, the court stated that "[t]he opportunity to participate in extracurricular activities is not, by and in itself, a property interest. . . . [Thus,] plaintiff would not be entitled to procedural due process."[108]

The *Pegram* court did leave open the theoretical possibility that exceptional circumstances might demand some due process before a student is excluded from extracurricular activities, reasoning that the principles of *Goss* extended to the total educational process, including participation in extracurricular activities.[109] The court did not indicate, however, what might constitute such exceptional circumstances, and other courts in the last two decades have refused to cloak extracurricular activities with the mantle of constitutional protection.

---

[104] C.B. *ex rel.* Breeding v. Driscoll, 82 F.3d 383 (11th Cir. 1996).
[105] 761 F. Supp. 45 (S.D. Tex. 1991).
[106] *Id.* at 47.
[107] 469 F. Supp. 1134 (M.D.N.C. 1979).
[108] *Id.* at 1139.
[109] *Id.*

In *Zehner v. Central Berkshire Regional School District,*[110] the federal district court characterized a student's interest in participating in high school athletics as a "mere expectation rather than a constitutionally protected claim of entitlement."[111] Thus, a suspension from athletic participation did not implicate the due process clause, even though it was linked to an accompanying academic suspension. Similarly, the court in *Bonner v. Lincoln Parish School Board*[112] held that an expulsion from the high school basketball team for violation of team rules, in addition to a suspension from school, was not of constitutional magnitude and did not require a due process hearing.[113] Comparable rulings have emerged outside the athletic arena.[114]

Some courts have considered suspensions from extracurricular activities after there had been some type of hearing. In those cases, the courts have not had to address the underlying issue of whether constitutional protections applied because even if the students' interests were protected, they received all the process that was due.[115]

Suspensions from extracurricular activities often accompany academic suspension. In such cases, the courts consistently have held that the addition of an extracurricular suspension does not entitle the student to more process than is required for the short-term academic suspension.[116] This is true even if the extracurricular suspension exceeds ten days. In the *Pegram* case cited above, the suspended student's parents did not object to the process given for the ten-day academic suspension, but instead argued that the

---

[110] 921 F. Supp. 850 (D. Mass. 1995).

[111] *Id.* at 862.

[112] 685 So. 2d 432 (La. App. 1996).

[113] *Id.* at 435.

[114] *See* Juran v. Independence or Cent. Sch. Dist. 13J, 898 F. Supp. 728 (D. Or. 1995) (denial of senior award following suspension did not violate due process); Bernstein v. Menard, 557 F. Supp. 90 (E.D. Va. 1982) (no property interest in school band membership); Jacob v. School Bd., 519 So. 2d 1002 (Fla. App. 1987) (upholding revocation of honor society membership).

[115] *See Zehner*, 921 F. Supp. at 862 (suspension of parking privileges most likely de minimis, but even if protected, sufficient due process where student given notice, reason for suspension, and opportunity to explain); Brands v. Sheldon Community Schs., 671 F. Supp. 627 (N.D. Ia. 1987) (wrestler declared ineligible for sexual misconduct afforded due process when given hearing and opportunity to present his side of story).

[116] *See* Donovan v. Ritchie, 68 F.3d 14 (1st Cir. 1995) (suspension from extracurricular activities, in addition to ten-day academic suspension, does not trigger more formal set of procedures); Manico v. South Colonie Cent. Sch. Dist., 584 N.Y.S.2d 519 (Sup. Ct. 1992) (upholding two-day extracurricular suspension in conjunction with academic suspension); Katchak v. Glasgow Indep. Sch. System, 690 F. Supp. 580 (W.D. Ky. 1988) (upholding five-day suspension from baseball team in conjunction with five-day academic suspension).

addition of a four-month suspension from extracurricular activities removed the case from the short-term suspension category and thus required more formal procedures.[117] The court rejected their contention. In a similar vein, the Third Circuit held in *Palmer v. Merluzzi*[118] that a student faced with a sixty-day athletic suspension was not entitled to more due process than was required for a ten-day academic suspension even though the athletic suspension might have jeopardized the student's opportunity for a college athletic scholarship.[119]

Even though procedural due process seldom constrains school officials in imposing extracurricular suspensions, they must be careful to adhere to local district policies. In a rare instance of a court striking down an extracurricular suspension, a New York court in *Manico v. South Colonie Central School District*[120] considered an athletic suspension imposed by an athletic director pursuant to his school's "Athletic Guide." The court concluded that the suspension was arbitrary because the Guide had not been adopted by the school board and the athletic director was not authorized to determine violations and impose penalties.[121]

In-School Suspension

For many students, an out-of-school suspension is the functional equivalent of an officially sanctioned school holiday. The child is free from the constraints of the schoolhouse and often has little or no supervision during the period of suspension, particularly in those families with parents who work outside the home.

The questionable benefits of such "discipline" become even more pronounced when the student's infraction is something like truancy, one of the major grounds for student suspension. An out-of-school suspension under such circumstances effectively rewards the very behavior the school is attempting to correct.[122]

For good reason, then, schools often turn to the "in-school suspension" as an alternative means of discipline. How much process, if any, is due a student who remains in school during a suspension? Several courts have addressed this issue.

---

[117] 469 F. Supp. at 1140.
[118] 868 F.2d 90 (3d Cir. 1989).
[119] *Id.* at 95-96.
[120] 584 N.Y.S.2d 519 (Sup. Ct. 1992).
[121] *Id.* at 522.
[122] *See generally* School Suspensions: Are They Helping Children?, Children's Defense Fund (1975).

In *Wise v. Pea Ridge School District*,[123] a student was given a three-day in-school suspension for excessive tardiness. The child's parents challenged the constitutionality of the suspension on the ground that the child was not provided with notice and a hearing prior to the suspension. The court, however, concluded that no such measures were required with an in-school suspension.[124]

Other courts have suggested that the key to determining whether notice and a hearing are required for an in-school suspension is whether the student is afforded *educational* opportunities during the period of suspension. In *Hayes v. Unified School District*,[125] a student received a five-day suspension for repeated misbehavior and was placed in a "timeout room" within the school building for the period of suspension. The child's parents sued in federal district court, claiming that the child was denied procedural due process because school officials held no hearing prior to the suspension. In rejecting the parents' claim, the court stated that procedural safeguards are required only when the school impinges on a student's interest in *education*. Because the student was given class assignments to work on in the time-out room, the student's education was not disrupted. Thus, said the court, there was no deprivation of a property or liberty interest to trigger procedural due process.[126]

In contrast, the court in *Cole v. Newton Special Municipal Separate School District*[127] concluded that a student's in-school suspension did violate procedural due process, in the absence of notice and a hearing, because the student was not given any school work during her six days of isolation from the rest of the school. The court summarized its position as follows:

> [T]he physical presence of a student at school is not conclusive as to whether school officials are excused from according a hearing in connection with imposing in-school isolation characterized by exclusion from the classroom. . . . Under certain circumstances, in-school isolation could well constitute as much of a deprivation of education as an at-home suspension. In other words, a student could be excluded from the educational process as much by be-

---

[123] 675 F. Supp. 1524 (W.D. Ark. 1987).
[124] *Id.* at 1531.
[125] 669 F. Supp. 1519 (D. Kan. 1987).
[126] *Id.* at 1528.
[127] 676 F. Supp. 749 (S.D. Miss. 1987), *aff'd*, 853 F.2d 924 (5th Cir. 1988).

> ing placed in isolation as by being barred from the school grounds. The primary thrust of the educational process is classroom instruction; in both situations the student is excluded from the classroom. This is not to say that any in-school detention would necessarily be equivalent to a suspension; it would depend on *the extent to which the student was deprived of instruction or the opportunity to learn.*[128]

Thus, if a suspended student is deprived of educational opportunities, procedural due process may be triggered, regardless of whether or not the student is physically present at school during the period of suspension. It bears repeating, however, that the principles of *Goss v. Lopez* do *not* apply if the deprivation is "*de minimis*."[129] Courts will not be inclined to scrutinize minor methods of classroom discipline, such as short "time outs," even if such measures deprive a student temporarily of the same educational opportunities as those enjoyed by the student's classmates. Indeed, the purpose of such measures often is to provide the disciplined child a unique "educational opportunity"—to think about the misbehavior that precipitated the punishment.

These principles came to the fore in *Dickens v. Johnson County Board of Education*,[130] a case in which a sixth-grader's parents claimed that placement of the child in a "time-out box," without a prior hearing, was unconstitutional because it deprived the child of his property interest in receiving a public education. The court upheld the disciplinary measure, noting that "not every use or even misuse of school discipline implicates the Fourteenth Amendment."[131] In the view of the court, the discipline was *de minimis* and thus did not trigger the protections of the due process clause. In concluding, the court commented: "[T]eachers should be free to impose minor forms of classroom discipline, such as admonishing students, requiring special assignments, restricting activities, and denying certain privileges, without being subjected to the strictures of due process scrutiny."[132]

---

[128] *Id.* at 751 (emphasis added). *See also* Alabama & Coushatta Tribes v. Trustees of Big Sandy Indep. Sch. Dist., 817 F. Supp. 1319 (E.D. Tex. 1993) (in-school suspension did not violate *substantive* due process when students afforded opportunity to pursue regular coursework and received instructional assistance).

[129] *Goss*, 419 U.S. at 576.

[130] 661 F. Supp. 155 (E.D. Tenn. 1987).

[131] *Id.* at 157.

[132] *Id. See also* Rasmus v. State of Ariz., 939 F. Supp. 709 (D. Ariz. 1996) (denying student ability to work on class assignment during a 10-minute time out *de minimis*).

School Bus Suspension

The courts' focus on the deprivation of *educational* opportunity also has influenced their jurisprudence on the suspension of students from riding the school bus. The leading case in this area remains *Rose v. Nashua Board of Education*,[133] in which the United States Court of Appeals for the First Circuit considered a suspension of bus transportation following repeated acts of vandalism. Because the bus drivers had to watch the road while transporting their passengers, they could not identify the specific students responsible for the vandalism. As a result, the school board approved a policy permitting the suspension of bus transportation, without any hearing, for continued acts of vandalism. When such acts occurred, several bus routes were suspended from operation for five days.

Parents of children who rode on the affected bus routes sued in federal court, claiming that their children were not responsible for the vandalism and were denied due process by the board's mass punishment. They argued that their children had a right to bus transportation under state law.[134]

The court rejected the parents' arguments, stating that the procedural protections required by *Goss* were meant for deprivations of educational opportunity. At stake here, said the court, was only the *de minimis* "inconvenience" of having to make alternative arrangements for transportation for five days. The court concluded:

> The fact that New Hampshire law guarantees free bus transportation does not seem sufficient to create a constitutionally protected interest in the *suspension-free* service that appellants seek. . . . [T]he deprivation itself caused only inconvenience, not loss of educational opportunity or other significant injury. We believe it is a "de minimis" deprivation that does not call for constitutional "[d]ue [p]rocess" protection.[135]

Some states do provide individual students with a right to a hearing prior to suspension from riding the bus,[136] but such policies appear to be the exception rather than the rule. Of course, it

---

[133] 679 F.2d 279 (1st Cir. 1982).

[134] *Id.* at 280-81.

[135] *Id.* at 282.

[136] *See, e.g.*, Ill. Comp. Stat. Ann. ch. 105, § 10-22.6(b).0

bears repeating that state law or even local school board policy can always extend more procedural due process to students than is required by the federal constitution.

Indefinite Suspensions

School officials sometimes will suspend a student indefinitely, pending some future action. Because of the uncertain duration of such suspensions, schools would be well advised to treat them as long-term, with all the rights that may attach. A federal court in Missouri, for example, held that a student is entitled to a *formal* hearing prior to an indefinite suspension pending a hearing on an expulsion recommendation.[137]

Occasionally, an indefinite suspension will be imposed to encourage parents to participate in the discipline process. The suspension may stand until the parents come to school for a conference or take some other action requested by school officials. In one early case, for example, a 15-year-old high school student who came to school intoxicated was suspended indefinitely until the student and her parents submitted to family counseling.[138] The principal felt the parents were at least partly responsible for their daughter's drinking. When the family challenged the suspension in a federal lawsuit, the court held in their favor, asserting that it was "fundamentally unfair to keep a student out of school indefinitely because of difficulties between the student and her parents, unless those difficulties manifest themselves in a real threat to school discipline."[139]

Thus, indefinite suspensions are legally suspect. Moreover, they may effectively place control over the duration of a suspension in the hands of students and their parents, which can present a host of practical problems for school officials.

---

[137] Hill v. Rankin County Sch. Dist., 843 F. Supp. 1112 (S.D. Miss. 1993).

[138] Cook v. Edwards, 341 F. Supp. 307 (D.N.H. 1972).

[139] *Id.* at 311.

Timeliness of Suspension

Ordinarily, the timeliness of a suspension is not at issue because the student is suspended immediately following the disciplinary hearing. What happens, however, if the misconduct giving rise to the suspension occurs at the end of the school year? Can the punishment be imposed in the next school term, weeks or perhaps months after the misconduct?

School officials would be advised to familiarize themselves with applicable state statutes and local policies prior to imposing such a delayed suspension. At least one court has concluded that school officials were precluded by state law from enforcing a suspension in the school year after that in which the student's misconduct occurred.[140]

Appealing a Short-Term Suspension

State law and local district policies also govern whether a student may appeal a short-term suspension decision. A student has no federal *constitutional* right to judicial review of such a decision or even to administrative review within the school district.[141]

Administrative review of a suspension decision, however, is common, and students may have a *right* to appeal based on state statute and/or district policy.[142] A typical route for the appeal is to the office of the superintendent, where either the superintendent or a hearing officer appointed by the superintendent will hear the appeal. In some cases, the board of education assumes the responsibility for reviewing the appeal. Even in these cases, however, a hearing officer (usually the superintendent or someone from the superintendent's staff) may represent the board at the appeals hearing. The evidence presented at the hearing is then summarized in the form of a report to the full board. After reviewing the report, the board makes a decision to uphold or reverse the suspension.[143]

---

[140] Rossman v. Conran, 572 N.E.2d 728 (Ohio App. 1988).

[141] Smith v. Severn, 129 F.3d 419, 429 (7th Cir. 1997) (school board review of three-day suspension "completely gratuitous" and not constitutionally required).

[142] *See, e.g.*, Richie v. Board of Educ., 933 S.W.2d 375 (Ark. 1996) (denial of right to appeal three-day suspension to school board was unlawful).

[143] *See, e.g.*, Ill. Comp. Stat. Ann. ch. 105, § 10-22.6(b).

A student's right to *judicial* review of a suspension decision is not as common. In a recent case, for example, a federal district court in Michigan held that under Michigan law, a student had no entitlement to judicial review of a school board's ten-day suspension. School district policy, moreover, provided for review only of expulsions.[144]

Judges generally are loath to interfere with the day-to-day decisions of school administrators. Thus, if state law is unclear as to whether a student has a right to judicial review of a short-term suspension, courts often will forgo review based on notions of public policy.[145] The high standard for judicial review established by an Alabama court provides a good example of such a hands-off policy: suspension decisions will not be reviewed except in the "rare case where there is a shocking disparity" between the student's offense and the penalty imposed.[146]

If a court does entertain a suspension appeal, the standard of review generally is deferential as well. In *Reasoner v. Meyer*,[147] the court stated that a court reviewing a suspension decision is required to follow a school board's credibility determinations and must engage in a strong presumption in favor of the validity of the board's decision.[148] In addition to considering the interests of the suspended student, a reviewing court will take into account the seriousness of the student's offense, the history of the student's past conduct, and the impact of the student's conduct on the education of other students.[149]

Finally, even if judicial review of a suspension decision is permitted by state law, a court generally will not review a case unless the suspended student first has pursued all possible appeal avenues within the school district. In other words, the student must exhaust all administrative remedies before seeking relief in the courts. For example, in *Webb v. Ironton City Schools*,[150] an Ohio statute allowed for an appeal of a principal's suspension decision

---

[144] Hartfield v. East Grand Rapids Pub. Schs., 960 F. Supp. 1259 (W.D. Mich. 1997). *See also* Boston v. Philpot, 645 F. Supp. 798, 805 (D. Kan. 1986) (three-day suspension not reviewable in federal court).

[145] *See, e.g.*, Byrd v. Irmo High Sch., 468 S.E.2d 861 (S.C. 1996) (short-term suspensions not appealable to circuit court, based on implicit language in expulsion statute and public policy).

[146] Scoggins v. Henry County Bd. of Educ., 549 So. 2d 99, 101 (Ala. Civ. App. 1989).

[147] 766 S.W.2d 161 (Mo. App. 1989).

[148] *Id.* at 164. *See also* Cross v. Princeton City Sch. Dist. Bd. of Educ., 550 N.E.2d 219 (Ohio Com. Pl. 1989) (10-day suspension for possession of drug paraphernalia upheld despite mitigating circumstances).

[149] Robinson v. Oak Park & River Forest High Sch., 571 N.E.2d 931, 935 (Ill. App. 1991).

[150] 686 N.E.2d 285 (Ohio App. 1996).

to the board of education. A student suspended by the principal bypassed the school board and challenged the principal's decision in court. An Ohio appellate court held, however, that the principal's decision was not a "final order" and thus was not reviewable by a court.[151]

Other Considerations

Beyond the technical legal requirements of the law of procedure for expulsions and suspensions, several related issues often arise. For example, does a disciplinary transfer to another school trigger the same protections as a suspension? What are the legal responsibilities of a school for the continued education of a student who has been suspended? Can a student's grades be reduced during the period of a suspension? Can a school expel or suspend a student for incidents occurring off school grounds? The following section addresses these issues, among others.

Disciplinary Transfers

School administrators sometimes handle problem students by transferring them out of their school rather than suspending them. Often these transfers are to "alternative" schools for students with behavior problems. The question is whether such a transfer is really a form of "backdoor" suspension. If so, are there procedural requirements that must be met before a student can be transferred?

It appears that there is no general rule in this area, and school officials will have to consult their local laws and policies. An early decision by a federal district court in Pennsylvania concluded that a disciplinary transfer must be preceded by the same procedural due process that is required prior to a short-term suspension, including notice and a hearing.[152] In supporting its holding, the court noted the trauma that a mid-year transfer could have on a child: "[T]he transfer of a pupil during a school year from a familiar

---

[151] *Id.* at 287.

[152] Everett v. Marcose, 426 F. Supp. 397 (E.D. Pa. 1977).

school to a strange and possibly more distant school would be a terrifying experience for many children of normal sensibilities."[153]

In *W.A.N. v. School Board*,[154] a Florida appellate court reached a similar result. In that case, parents challenged their son's involuntary transfer to a school for children with behavioral problems. School officials made the transfer decision without notice or a hearing, and asserted that procedural due process was not required because the transfer was not a suspension. The court held for the parents, stating that the school district's distinction between transfers and suspensions was more semantical than substantive: "[W]e are persuaded that any distinction between the terms is meaningless. . . . The fact of and consequences flowing from the transfer disclose all of the definitional elements associated with a statutory suspension."[155]

On the other hand, a more recent Colorado decision held that a student's reassignment to another school for 90 days for alcohol use was *not* the legal equivalent of a suspension for more than five days, which would have triggered a statutory hearing requirement.[156] Challenges to disciplinary transfers on substantive due process grounds also have failed.[157]

Thus, the law on disciplinary transfers is inconsistent. To be on the safe side, school officials probably would be well-advised to treat such transfers as suspensions, at least for procedural due process purposes.

Responsibility for Alternative Education

The courts are also split on the issue of whether schools must provide some form of alternative education for students on suspension or expulsion. From an educator's standpoint, such schooling would seem desirable, but it is common practice nonetheless to provide no alternative education for students removed from school for disciplinary reasons. Perhaps underlying this practice is the thought that the loss of schooling, including examination grades, extracurricular activities, and even social events, should be part of the punishment for the student's misbehavior.

---

153 *Id.* at 400

154 504 So. 2d 529 (Fla. Dist. Ct. App. 1987).

155 *Id.* at 530.

156 Martinez v. School Dist. No. 60, 852 P.2d 1275 (Colo. App. 1992).

157 *See* C.B. *ex rel.* Breeding v. Driscoll, 82 F.3d 383 (11th Cir. 1996).

Several courts have concluded that schools have no legal responsibility to provide alternative education for suspended or expelled students. In *Matter of Jackson*,[158] for example, a student was expelled for the remainder of the school year for physically assaulting another student and a teacher. In a juvenile proceeding following the expulsion, the judge ordered the school district to provide an alternative educational program for the expelled student. The school district challenged the decision on appeal, and the appellate court held in the district's favor, concluding that "public schools have no affirmative duty to provide an alternative educational program for suspended students in the absence of a legislative mandate."[159]

As the *Jackson* court's statement suggests, of course, state legislation may require alternative educational programs for suspended or expelled students. In *F.N. ex rel. D.N. v. Board of Education*,[160] a federal district court held that a New York statute requires school districts to take immediate steps for alternative education for students suspended more than five days. Similarly, a federal district court in New Mexico held that suspended students have at least a provisional right to continue their education and that suspensions must be accompanied by procedures sufficient to protect that right.[161]

The legislative mandate for alternative education may arise implicitly, through state compulsory attendance laws. In a recent Mississippi case, for example, the court held that a school district policy of refusing to allow suspended students to attend an alternative educational program and then treating the students' absences from the regular school program as unexcused was arbitrary and capricious under compulsory attendance laws and void as against public policy.[162] On the other hand, other state courts have concluded that their compulsory attendance laws do *not* require educational alternatives for properly suspended or expelled students.[163]

It does seem clear that suspended or expelled students have no federal constitutional right to an alternative education.[164] State constitutions, however, may provide students with greater rights

---

[158] 352 S.E.2d 449 (N.C. Ct. App. 1987).

[159] *Id.* at 455.

[160] 894 F. Supp. 605 (E.D.N.Y. 1995).

[161] Bivens *ex rel.* Green v. Albuquerque Pub. Schs., 899 F. Supp. 556 (D.N.M. 1995).

[162] In Interest of T.H., 681 So. 2d 110 (Miss. 1996).

[163] Board of Educ. v. School Comm., 612 N.E.2d 666 (Mass. 1993); Walter v. School Bd., 518 So. 2d 1331 (Fla. App. 1987).

[164] *See* Craig v. Selma City Sch. Bd., 801 F. Supp. 585 (S.D. Ala. 1992) (rejecting substantive due process claim); Doe v. Superintendent of Schs., 653 N.E.2d 1088 (Mass. 1995) (same).

than those afforded under the United States Constitution. One state court has found such a state constitutional basis for requiring alternative education, at least in the case of a lengthy suspension or expulsion. In *Phillip Leon M. v. Greenbrier County Bd. of Educ.*,[165] the Supreme Court of West Virginia considered the expulsion of a student for one year for possession of a firearm. The court held that a state constitutional provision requiring a "thorough and efficient system of free schools" gave the student a right to an alternative educational program during the expulsion period. To refuse such an alternative, concluded the court, would not be "narrowly tailored" to meet the school's objective of providing a safe and secure school environment.[166]

Grade Reduction as Part of Suspension

In most jurisdictions, students do not have a right to make up work missed during an out-of-school suspension.[167] Thus, a natural consequence of the student's absence from class may be a grade reduction. But what if a school assesses a grade reduction or other academic penalty over and above that which would normally occur as a result of the student's absence? Some school districts, in an effort to curb student misbehavior, have adopted policies that automatically reduce the grades of a suspended student. Such policies have been challenged in several cases, with mixed results.

It is certainly appropriate (and legal) for a school to assess an academic penalty, such as an "F" in a course, for academic misconduct, such as cheating on an exam.[168] The tougher question is whether it is appropriate to impose an academic penalty for non-academic misconduct. Two cases in which students were suspended for drinking alcohol on school-sponsored trips provide a good illustration of both the difficult issues involved and the differing views among courts.

---

[165] 484 S.E.2d 909 (W. Va. 1996).

[166] *Id.* at 914-16.

[167] *But see* Katzman v. Cumberland Valley Sch. Dist., 479 A.2d 671, 674 (Pa. Commw. Ct. 1984) (Pennsylvania statute evidences legislative intent that "educational make up be provided to a student for exams and work missed while being disciplined by temporary or full suspension").

[168] *See, e.g.*, Reed v. Vermilion Local Sch. Dist., 614 N.E.2d 1101, 1102-03 (Ohio App. 1992).

In *New Braunfels Independent School District v. Armke*,[169] two high school seniors were suspended for three days for using alcohol on a school-sponsored trip. In addition to the suspension, the students received zeroes on all graded class work for each day of the three-day suspension and a three-grade-point deduction from their six-week grade averages for each day of suspension. The students challenged the grade penalties, arguing that imposition of an academic penalty for nonacademic behavior was unconstitutional. The court rejected the students' claims, holding that the grade reductions would not adversely impact either the students' property rights to an education or their reputations.[170]

One year later, a Pennsylvania court decided a similar case in favor of a student. In *Katzman v. Cumberland Valley School District*,[171] an eleventh-grade student was suspended for five days for alcohol use on a school trip. In addition, the school imposed a grade-reduction policy in which the student's grades in all classes were reduced by two percentage points for each day of the suspension. In contrast to the *Armke* decision, the *Katzman* court was troubled by what it viewed as the school's misrepresentation of the student's academic achievement. "Misrepresentation of achievement," said the court, "is . . . improper and . . . illegal whether the achievement is misrepresented by upgrading or by downgrading, if either is done for reasons that are irrelevant to the achievement being graded."[172]

More recent cases are equally inconsistent. In *Smith v. School City of Hobart*,[173] a federal district court in Indiana held that a grade reduction for each day of a student's suspension for alcohol use violated substantive due process. Such a penalty, concluded the court, was arbitrary because grades should reflect *academic* achievement.[174] In *In Interest of T.H.*,[175] however, a Mississippi court held that giving a student an F in all subjects for the semester did not violate substantive due process, even for a single, minor rule infraction.

---

[169] 658 S.W.2d 330 (Tex. Ct. App. 1983).

[170] *Id.* at 332 (citing Fisher v. Burkburnett Indep. Sch. Dist., 419 F. Supp. 1200 (N.D. Tex. 1976)).

[171] 479 A.2d 671 (Pa. Commw. Ct. 1984).

[172] *Id.* at 675.

[173] 811 F. Supp. 391 (N.D. Ind. 1993).

[174] *Id.* at 399. *See also* State *ex rel.* Yarber v. McHenry, 915 S.W.2d 325 (Mo. 1995) (loss of semester's credit a significant infringement on student's property interest, requiring a hearing).

[175] 681 So. 2d 110 (Miss. 1996).

Thus, whether academic penalties may be imposed for non-academic misbehavior currently is dependent on the law of the local jurisdiction. It does seem likely that a court that feels strongly about providing alternative education for suspended students also will be reluctant to allow school districts to impose automatic grade reductions whenever a student is suspended.

Expulsion or Suspension for Off-School Behavior

Whether a school has the authority to expel or suspend a student for behavior away from school generally depends on both the nature of the offense and the extent to which the off-school behavior affects what happens in school. In other words, unless the offense is quite serious, school officials will not have the authority to suspend a student unless they establish some nexus between the student's off-premises behavior and a potential disruption of the educational process at school.

For example, in *Robinson v. Oak Park & River Forest High School,*[176] the court held that expulsion of a student for a fight off school grounds after school hours was an abuse of discretion because there was no evidence to sugggest that the fight disrupted the school process. Similarly, in *Klein v. Smith,*[177] a high school student was suspended for ten days for "giving the finger" to a teacher while the teacher sat in his car at a restaurant parking lot after school hours. Even though a school rule prohibited vulgar or discourteous conduct toward a teacher, the court ruled that the suspension was unlawful because there was no connection between the off-school behavior and the two persons' roles "on school premises." At the time of the interaction, the teacher was not acting in his professional role as teacher, nor was the student acting in his role as student.[178]

The requisite connection between a student's off-school behavior and a possible disruption of the educational process is important even in the case of more serious offenses, such as drug

---

[176] 571 N.E.2d 931 (Ill. App. 1991).

[177] 635 F. Supp. 1440 (D. Me. 1986).

[178] *Id.* at 1441. While the court expressed disappointment at the student's behavior, it said, "The First Amendment protection of freedom of expression may not be made a casualty of the effort to force-feed good manners to the ruffians among us." *Id.* at 1442.

use. In *Anable v. Ford*,[179] a 12-year-old junior high school student was expelled for using marijuana. The student had consented to a urinalysis which indicated the use of marijuana, but school officials did not establish that the use occurred on school grounds. In striking down the expulsion, the court stated that the school's policy, which prohibited marijuana use by students regardless of place, was "an improper attempt by school officials to regulate off-campus conduct unrelated to school order or discipline."[180]

Of course, courts do have their limits, and if a student's off-school misconduct is sufficiently egregious, school administrators will be given more latitude in imposing suspensions and expulsions. In *Howard v. Colonial School District*,[181] a Delaware court upheld discipline against a student drug dealer, noting that the mere fact that the student's drug sales occurred off school grounds did not render the school board powerless to act. Similarly, in *Smith v. Little Rock School District*,[182] the court upheld the expulsion of a student who had been charged by the police with a murder that occurred away from school. In reaching its decision, the court used a balancing test:

> [T]he Court must balance the harm plaintiff may suffer as a result of his expulsion against the serious risk to other students which would be presented by plaintiff's presence at the school. The Court finds that the risk of harm to other students and the potential for disruption of educational processes outweigh whatever harm Smith may suffer as a result of his expulsion.[183]

School officials need not be *certain* prior to an expulsion or suspension that a student's off-school behavior will disrupt the educational process. Courts generally defer to the judgment of educators in assessing the need for discipline. This posture is illustrated by the following quote from *Pollnow v. Glennon*,[184] a case in which a student challenged his five-day suspension on the

---

[179] 653 F. Supp. 22 (W.D. Ark. 1985).
[180] *Id.* at 40. The court lauded the school's efforts to curtail student drug use, but concluded that off-school use "is within the realm of parents and law enforcement officials, not teachers and educational administrators." *Id.*
[181] 621 A.2d 362 (Del. Super. 1992).
[182] 582 F. Supp. 159 (E.D. Ark. 1984).
[183] *Id.* at 162.
[184] 594 F. Supp. 220 (S.D.N.Y. 1984), *aff'd*, 757 F.2d 496 (2d Cir. 1985).

ground that it was based on behavior that occurred away from school:

> Whether discipline is to be meted out to such students, and the measure thereof, is within the discretion of the school authorities. The mere fact that such conduct occurs . . . outside the school . . . does not preclude the *possibility* that such conduct . . . *may* adversely affect the educative process or endanger the health, safety or morals of pupils within the education system for which the school authorities are responsible. The school authorities are in the best position to determine whether the education system for which they are responsible has been or *could be* so affected, and their determination will not be upset absent some showing that they have abused their discretion in making it.[185]

In *Smith*, the court also upheld the validity of a school district policy allowing suspension or expulsion of a student based on "[c]riminal offenses committed away from school which *may* affect the school climate."[186] Of course, the seriousness of the alleged offense in *Smith* (murder) mitigated in favor of expulsion. Moreover, in light of the nature of the criminal charge, the court did not find persuasive the student's argument that he could not be disciplined until he had actually been convicted of the crime. If school officials "were forced to wait for a courtroom adjudication before taking action," said the court, "the rule would be meaningless."[187]

Sometimes a student's off-school behavior clearly will have a disruptive effect on the educational process. In *Donovan v. Ritchie*,[188] a student's off-campus conduct in copying an abusive and obscene description of other students ultimately led to widespread distribution of the document *at school*. Under those circumstances, the First Circuit had little difficulty concluding that the student's conduct was suspendable.

A final issue that has arisen in this area is whether a student may be suspended or expelled for misconduct at a school other than that in which the student is enrolled. A California appellate court answered in the affirmative in *Fremont Union High School*

---

[185] *Id.* at 224 (emphasis added).

[186] 582 F. Supp. at 159 (emphasis added).

[187] *Id.* at 161.

[188] 68 F.3d 14 (1st Cir. 1995).

District v. Santa Clara County Board of Education.[189] In that case a student had used a stun gun on a student at another school, so the egregiousness of the conduct may have warranted discipline even if the conduct had not occurred on the grounds of a school.

Double Jeopardy

Often a student's misbehavior is also a criminal offense, which may result in delinquency or criminal proceedings in addition to a suspension or expulsion from school. In several cases, students have argued that they may not be subject to both criminal prosecution and suspension or expulsion for the same conduct because such double punishment would violate notions of double jeopardy.

The courts uniformly have rejected such arguments on the ground that expulsions or suspensions are remedial in nature and not "punishment" for double jeopardy purposes.[190] Therefore, school officials may expel or suspend students without regard to prior or pending delinquency or criminal proceedings on the same conduct.[191]

First Amendment

Students sometimes challenge suspensions on the ground that the conduct for which they were suspended is protected by the First Amendment. Two cases, for example, involved students who distributed unofficial publications at school. In one case, the student's "newspaper" advocated violence against teachers.[192] In the other case, the student's publication advocated urination on school floors, garbage throwing, graffiti, and other damage to school property.[193]

While the courts recognize the importance of free speech in schools, student expression which constitutes a threat of material and substantial disruption to the educational process will not be protected by the cloak of the First Amendment. In both of the above cases, the students' short-term suspensions were upheld because the courts found the publications to have constituted such a threat.

---

[189] 286 Cal. Rptr. 915 (Cal. App. 1991).

[190] *In re* Phillips, 497 S.E.2d 292 (N.C. App. 1998); State v. Knutson, 946 P.2d 789 (Wash. App. 1997).

[191] Schank v. Hegele, 521 N.E.2d 9 (Ohio Comm. Pl. 1987).

[192] Bystrom v. Fridley High Sch., 686 F. Supp. 1387 (D. Minn.), *aff'd*, 855 F.2d 855 (1988).

[193] Board of Educ. v. Commissioner of Educ., 690 N.E.2d 480 (N.Y. 1997).

School officials must weigh all the circumstances to determine whether a student's expressive conduct is likely to cause a substantial disruption in the school. A final, recent example comes from South Carolina, where a middle school student was suspended for wearing a jacket depicting the Confederate battle flag. The federal district court in that case upheld the suspension, stating that in light of several recent incidents of racial tension at the school, wearing the jacket was likely to cause a disruption. Therefore, the suspension did not violate the First Amendment.[194]

Penalties for Wrongful Expulsions and Suspensions

Failure to provide the necessary due process when students are removed from school is a violation of the Fourteenth Amendment. Students and their parents may sue under 42 U.S.C. § 1983 for violation of a federal constitutional right. School districts may be sued under section 1983 if a district policy, practice, or custom—whether written or unwritten—is alleged to be unconstitutional.[195] School districts may not be held liable, however, for the acts of employees who violate student's constitutional rights contrary to district policy. Nor may school districts be liable for punitive damages under section 1983.[196]

Teachers or school administrators may be sued as individuals under section 1983, and they may be subject to punitive damages if they are found to have intentionally violated a student's constitutional rights.[197]

To recover damages from either a school district or individual district employees, a student must show actual damages. In *Carey v. Piphus*,[198] a high school student who was suspended for twenty days without due process sued under section 1983. He did not show actual damages, but argued that injury may be "presumed" to flow from every denial of procedural due process. The Supreme Court rejected the student's argument:

> [I]t is not reasonable to assume that every departure from procedural due process, no matter what the circumstances

---

194 Phillips v. Anderson County Sch. Dist. 5, 987 F. Supp. 488 (D.S.C. 1997).
195 Monell v. Department of Social Services, 436 U.S. 658 (1978).
196 *See* City of Newport v. Fact Concerts, Inc., 453 U.S. 247 (1981); Keson v. Talley Sch. Dist., 570 F. Supp. 408 (D.N.D. 1983).
197 Wells v. Haico Ind. Sch. Dist., 736 F.2d 243 (5th Cir. 1984).
198 435 U.S. 247 (1978).

> or how minor, inherently is as likely to cause distress . . . . Where the deprivation of a protected interest is substantially justified but procedures are deficient in some respect, there may well be those who suffer no distress over the procedural irregularities.[199]

Thus, a student who is suspended without procedural due process may have a remedy under section 1983 against the school district and any school employees who were party to the suspension. However, the student must establish an unlawful policy, practice, or custom to prevail against a school district, and the student must be prepared to produce evidence of actual damages, such as psychiatric testimony that the student was mentally affected by the suspension.

Substantive Due Process

A suspension or expulsion decision can be challenged on substantive due process grounds even if school officials have provided a student with proper notice, a hearing, and all other procedural protections. Substantive due process is not easy to define, but is grounded in notions of "fundamental fairness."[200] In the student expulsion/suspension context, fundamental fairness generally consists of two basic principles: (1) that the "punishment fit the crime," and (2) that "fair warning" be given to students so they know what behavior may result in suspension or expulsion.

Several early cases focused on the latter principle, particularly when school policies or regulations were vague. For example, in *Galveston Independent School District v. Boothe*,[201] a high school student was expelled for a full quarter after being caught with a small amount of marijuana off school grounds. Because the administrative regulation on which the expulsion was based prohibited the possession of marijuana "in our schools," the court held that the regulation did not clearly give students fair warning that possession off school grounds could result in expulsion. In reinstating the student, the court said, "Before a student can be punished by expulsion for violation of a school rule, regulation, or policy, it

---

[199] *Id.* at 263.

[200] *See* Cook v. Edwards, 341 F. Supp. 307 (D.N.H. 1972).

[201] 590 S.W.2d 553 (Tex. App. 1979).

must fairly apprise him of the type of prohibited conduct by which he may be expelled."[202]

No firm guidelines exist as to how specific school rules and regulations must be in order to give "fair warning" to students. School officials should operate on basic standards of reasonableness, such as the following standard set forth by a federal district court nearly thirty years ago:

> School rules probably do not need to be as narrow as criminal statutes, but if school officials contemplate severe punishment they must do so on the basis of a rule which is drawn so as to reasonably inform the student what specific conduct is proscribed. Basic notions of justice and fair play require that no person shall be made to suffer for a breach unless standards of behavior have first been announced, for who is to decide what has been breached?[203]

In recent years, most of the substantive due process challenges to suspensions and expulsions have focused on the first principle—that the "punishment fit the crime." Courts vary in their individual formulations of the standard, but the bottom line is that a student bringing a substantive due process claim bears a heavy burden, and consequently, few such claims succeed.

The Nebraska Supreme Court recently framed the substantive due process standard for student disciplinary proceedings as follows: there cannot be a "shocking disparity between the punishment and the offense."[204] Other courts have stated that substantive due process is violated only in the "rare case" in which "no rational relationship" exists between the punishment and the offense.[205] Still other courts give short shrift to substantive due process claims by simply asserting that such claims apply only when "fundamental rights" are infringed, and students have no fundamental right to education.[206]

---

[202] *Id.* at 557.

[203] Sullivan v. Houston Indep. Sch. Dist., 307 F. Supp. 1328, 1344-45 (S.D. Tex. 1969). *See also* Kelly v. Metropolitan County Bd. of Educ., 293 F. Supp. 385, 393 (M.D. Tenn. 1968) ("[t]he imposition of penalties in the absence of prescribed standards of conduct is contrary to our basic sense of justice").[204] Kolesnick v. Omaha Pub. Sch. Dist., 558 N.W.2d 807, 813-14 (Neb. 1997) (finding no such disparity for two-semester expulsion for possession of knife).

[205] James v. Unified Sch. Dist. No. 512, 899 F. Supp. 530, 534 (D. Kan. 1995) (finding rational relationship between expulsion and weapon possession); Hill v. Rankin County, Miss., Sch. Dist., 843 F. Supp. 1112 (S.D. Miss. 1993); Doe v. Superintendent of Schs., 653 N.E.2d 1088 (Mass. 1995).

[206] C.B. *ex rel.* Breeding v. Driscoll, 82 F.3d 383 (11th Cir. 1996); Craig v. Selma City Sch. Bd., 801 F. Supp. 585 (S.D. Ala. 1992); Doe v. Superintendent of Schs., 653 N.E.2d 1088 (Mass. 1995).

Thus, regardless of the particular standard employed, courts are extremely deferential to school officials in reviewing particular punishments for particular offenses. A sampling of substantive due process cases in the last decade shows the following: neither a five-day nor a nine-day suspension implicates substantive due process;[207] expulsion for weapons possession does not violate substantive due process;[208] a five-day suspension from school and extracurricular activities for drinking at a school event does not violate substantive due process;[209] and a three-day in-school suspension for excessive tardies does not violate substantive due process.[210]

In one rare case, a federal district court in Indiana did find a substantive due process violation when a school district imposed an automatic grade reduction for each day of a student's suspension for alcohol use.[211] The court in that case felt that imposition of an academic penalty for a nonacademic offense was arbitrary. As we noted previously,[212] however, that decision by no means represents a general rule.

School officials should use care to ensure that students are given fair notice of disciplinary rules, and that punishment is not grossly disproportionate to a student's offense. On the other hand, they should be aware that their vulnerability to a substantive due process claim is limited.

CONCLUSION

Since the *Goss* decision in 1975, providing students with their rights has occupied the minds of many. The law of expulsion and suspension has reached a level of complexity that no longer can school officials simply "do what is right" when punishing students by expulsion or suspension. School officials must know the law. Hopefully, the law of student expulsion and suspension can be the same as "doing what is right" and thus help support the school in controlling student behavior while simultaneously respecting the rights of students.

---

[207] Kicklighter v. Evans County Sch. Dist., 968 F. Supp. 712 (S.D. Ga. 1997) (five-day suspension); C.B. *ex rel.* Breeding v. Driscoll, 82 F.3d 383 (11th Cir. 1996) (nine-day suspension).

[208] James v. Unified Sch. Dist. No. 512, 899 F. Supp. 530 (D. Kan. 1995); Kolesnick v. Omaha Pub. Sch. Dist., 558 N.W.2d 807 (Neb. 1997); Doe v. Superintendent of Schs., 653 N.E.2d 1088 (Mass. 1995).

[209] Katchak v. Glasgow Indep. Sch. Sys., 690 F. Supp. 580 (W.D. Ky. 1988).

[210] Wise v. Pea Ridge Sch. Dist. No. 109, 855 F.2d 560 (8th Cir. 1988).

[211] Smith v. School City of Hobart, 811 F. Supp. 391 (N.D. Ind. 1993).

[212] *See supra* text accompanying notes 167-55.